The Strategic Newcomer

The Immigrant's Practical Guide to Thriving, Belonging, and Becoming

Isaac O. Ebhohimhen

Paperback ISBN: 978-1-963732-17-7
Hardcover ISBN: 978-1-963732-18-4

Published by

The Publishing Pad
www.thepublishingpad.com

What People Are Saying

"This should be a mandatory reading for anyone immigrating. It's the mentor every newcomer deserves."
—Rev. Rob Nylen, Senior Pastor, RiverCross Church

"This is a gift many immigrants didn't know they needed but will be so glad they found."
—Sophia Etuhube, Award-winning Journalist, Coach, Mentor

"As a newcomer, I could immediately relate to his story.... It will be an invaluable source of inspiration for many of us who are here and the many who will come after us."
—Celeste Dean, Newcomer

"The Strategic Newcomer is an excellent resource for individuals and families seeking to not only settle but flourish in their new environment."
— Pastor William Folarin Onososen, Senior Pastor, Redeemed Christian Church of God, Saint John

"This is a tremendous resource for employers, community leaders, newcomers, and anyone interested in assisting newcomers acclimatize to a new environment."
—Jim Kokocki, 2015-2016 International President, Toastmasters International

"The Strategic Newcomer is more than a guide; it's a heartfelt, courageous, and genuine resource for anyone navigating any new beginning."
—**Glen Fillmore,** Vice President, Strategic Growth and Transformation, Saint John Energy.

"… The Strategic Newcomer is the essential guide for any professional starting a new chapter. It's the perfect carry-on for a successful journey, making sure you don't just arrive, but truly take off in your career."
—**Chris Weir,** Sales and Business Development Professional | MBA Sales Instructor | Axis Co-founder and Sales Coach in Residence

"Isaac O. Ebhohimhen has written an important book that would serve new-comers as a survival guide. It will also be useful to cultural humility coaches as a reference material, providing perspective on the significant sacrifices newcomers make to successfully integrate in new countries."
—**Sochi Azuh,** Podcaster & Communication Specialist | Saint John New-comers Centre

Dedication

To the Almighty God for his goodness, mercy, and love

and

To every newcomer or immigrant who dared to dream beyond borders.

Table of Contents

Acknowledgements

This book would not have been possible without the support, encouragement, and contributions of many incredible people.

First, to my wife, Evelyn, and to our champs, Emmanuel, Nancy, and Eva, thank you for your unwavering support. Your love, patience, and sacrifices have shaped the person I am today.

To my parents, your strength and resilience inspired every word of this book.

To my siblings, thank you for being my sounding board and constant source of motivation.

To my mentors, colleagues, and friends, your insights, feedback, and encouragement gave this project life. I'm especially grateful to those who shared their own newcomer experiences with me. Your stories added depth and meaning beyond what I could have created alone.

To Chisom Ezeh and her team at The Publishing Pad, thank you for the guidance and motivation to complete this project.

To the reader who has picked up this book, thank you for your curiosity and trust. Whether you are an immigrant or newcomer, a supporter of immigrants, or someone simply seeking to understand the journey, I hope this book serves as both a guide and a companion.

Finally, to every newcomer striving for success, this book is for you. Your courage and determination continue to inspire the world.

Foreword

Moving to a new country is one of the most profound decisions anyone could make. As I interact with newcomers every day, I can tell you that it is a journey characterized by bravery and hope. This book is a companion for that journey. It portrays the emotional weight and practical realities of starting over in a new land and answers the silent questions that keep many up at night. With empathy, passion, and insight, it offers a roadmap to help newcomers move from survival to stability and from uncertainty to confidence.

What makes this book powerful is its honesty, practical insights, and incredibly relatable reflections. It does not sugarcoat the newcomer experience, but it also does not dwell in despair. Instead, it highlights the tools that help newcomers rise.

Above all, this book is a reminder that every immigrant journey is both deeply personal and profoundly universal. The challenges may be different, but the longing for belonging, success, and purpose is the same. As you read, you'll find not only guidance but also the courage to keep going and inspiration to give back. Let these pages teach, reassure, and remind you that you are not alone.

Whether you are a recent newcomer or someone who supports the newcomer's integration journey, this book will serve as a guide, a mirror, and a source of hope. Every story shared and lesson learned is a testament to the strength of the human spirit.

Mohamed Bagha
Managing Director, Saint John Newcomers Centre, NB, Canada

Introduction

There's a quiet kind of bravery in packing your life into two suitcases and boarding a flight to the unknown. For many immigrants or newcomers, that moment is both tender and terrifying, and it's where this story begins.

You don't really believe it's happening until the plane takes off and the ground you've always known begins to shrink beneath the clouds. Then home becomes just a collection of lights far below your window, and suddenly you realize you're on your way to a place where your name sounds foreign, your favorite dishes are considered "exotic," and your stories might need subtitles.

They say leaving is a choice, but that's too simple. For me, it wasn't just about going; it was about everything I had to leave behind. I was trading familiarity for the unknown and comfort for curiosity. I had no idea what would greet me on the other side of the ocean. I didn't know if I'd fit in, stand out, fall apart, or rise. Yet I was leaving, not because I didn't love my home but because I wanted to know what else was possible. Something inside me needed to grow beyond the borders I'd always known. All I knew was that I couldn't stay. I wanted more. I needed more. And that was enough of a springboard to launch me into a new adventure.

This book is for those who've felt that same ache, that tension between gratitude for everything that has shaped you and hunger for something more. It's for the dreamers, the seekers, the parents making difficult choices in the interest of their children, and the young adults carrying the weight of generations on their shoulders. If you've ever stood at a crossroads and whispered, "There has to be more than this," then this book is for you.

I didn't have all the answers, but I knew I couldn't stay where I was.
So, I moved forward, not with certainty, but with hope and faith in God.

This book isn't just about crossing borders. It's about what gets left behind and what you discover when you land. It's about starting over when you didn't even know you were ending. It's about the quiet heartbreak of goodbye and the louder, messier miracle of hello.

Maybe that's where all newcomers' stories should begin: not at the airport, not in the visa office, not even in the daydreams but in that sharp, aching question: *Can I stay here? Is this truly El Dorado or an exercise in futility? What if I made a mistake? What if I don't fit here? What happens next?*

This book is about what happens next. For me, it's a story of cold winters and warm strangers, of jobs that paid little and taught much, of the loneliness that pressed in like a second skin on some nights, and of the resilience that bloomed anyway. It's about my first grocery trip, my first real friendship in a new land, and the way I learned to carry two cultures without dropping either. You will read not just my story but stories from several other newcomers who generously contributed their experiences to this book.

This book is for the newcomer trying to understand a foreign culture, the international student adjusting to life far from home, the skilled worker rebuilding a career from scratch, and the parent working multiple jobs to give their children opportunities they never had.

It's also for the family members who experience unexpected culture shock in a new environment, where everything they once knew has been left behind and the pain of separation from the familiar runs deep. For example, how do you explain to your ten-year-old daughter who was already in junior secondary 1 (equivalent to grade 7) that she now has to drop down two classes and start over in grade 5 because the education system in your new country is different from what you knew back home?

In this book, I use the terms *immigrant* and *newcomer* interchangeably. Immigration happens in different ways and for different reasons. Perhaps you are the spouse of a military officer and you're moving to join them on a new posting, or a young adult leaving your familiar environment to further your education in another city or country. If you have moved or will ever move from one location to another, you are or will be an immigrant, and I have you in mind.

Or maybe you're just curious about what it's really like to start over in a place where no one knows your name or, worse, can pronounce it. Wherever you are, this story is for you, for the ones who left, the ones who stayed, and the ones still deciding.

In this book, you'll find stories—mine and those of others—woven through different chapters. They are stories of doubt and courage, of challenges and triumphs. Each chapter relays a part of my journey and experiences. It's not a straight line; it's a winding path full of obstacles, triumphs, and beautiful surprises. My hope is that these stories will remind you you're not alone.

This book isn't just about migrating, facing challenges in your journey, or even receiving permanent residency or citizenship in your new country. It's about what you do with it. The real story is in what comes after: the becoming, the rebuilding, the purpose.

By the end of this book, you will feel not only inspired but also equipped. You will better understand the unwritten rules of thriving in a new country, learn how to rebuild your confidence and career, and discover the power of your own voice in a land that is waiting to hear your story.

You are not just starting over. You are becoming.

Let's begin.

CHAPTER ONE

Stepping into the Unknown

*"Jump off the cliff and learn how
to make wings on the way down."*
—RAY BRADBURY

It was December 12, 2022. As the sun set in the city of Lagos, western Nigeria, I packed my entire life and career into two big suitcases and a backpack. I was headed to Murtala Muhammed International Airport in Lagos to begin my journey to Canada.

It had taken me over three years to decide whether to remain in my comfort zone, with a flourishing career in the Nigerian oil and gas industry and a thriving family business, or to relocate to Canada to further my studies and find new international opportunities.

My career in Nigeria spans more than a decade in oil and gas, engineering, operations, IT, supply chain, and facilities management. I began as a field engineer intern at International Payment Devices Limited (IPDL) in 2006. Thereafter, I joined GCA Energy Limited as an application engineer and rose through the ranks to become the operations manager. In 2017, I resigned to join Aiteo Eastern Exploration and Production Company Limited (AEEPCo), one of Nigeria's largest indigenous oil and gas companies, which owned what was likely the country's longest swamp pipeline, spanning over one hundred kilometers.

I led multiple projects, served as a regulatory liaison, and became an industry thought leader in crude oil and gas measurement and project management. I was living in a five-bedroom duplex with a two-bedroom Boys Quarter (BQ) in a luxury residential estate, and everything else was going well. So why did I give up all of that for a journey to the unknown? Because something inside me needed to grow beyond the borders I had always known. I knew I couldn't stay. I wanted more out of life. I needed more. But there were many other reasons it took me so long to make the decision.

The first of these reasons was family. I am the fifth child of six siblings with a widowed mother. We are a closely knit family, constantly visiting each other. I share a very close bond with my aged mother. In fact, after my dad passed in November 2020, she moved in to live with me for over a year, and our relationship became even stronger.

My wife is her mother's only child, so I became the dearest son to my mother-in-law. Leaving both my mother and my parents-in-law behind without the opportunity to see them regularly was a burden that, for a long time, I was not ready to bear.

Professionally, I was also tied down. I was leading the metering scope of a critical project, and I didn't want to walk away from an organization where my colleagues had become more like friends and family. I felt a strong sense of responsibility to see the projects through to completion.

Beyond work, I had deep community ties as a Christian, a volunteer, and a mentor to students and young couples. In church, I had just handed over my role as prayer secretary to be the head of personnel. I was also a Sunday school teacher and an active member of the Men's Missionary Union (MMU). In my residential estate, I was serving as the Zone A1 secretary and the chief whip for the general estate. I was part of the team responsible in reinventing the estate in line with modern technology for communication, infrastructure development, and security.

There was so much going on in my life. Leaving all of that behind would be a battle for me. Now you see why I had reservations.

As someone who has been a product of God's mercies and grace all my life, I also needed to be sure He was leading me to relocate abroad. This confirmation was important to me because knowing that God was with me meant everything to me. It would give me an assurance that He would guide me through and bless me, and if things got tough, I could confidently turn to Him for help, knowing that He had asked me to go! So, I spent time praying for clarity. Then one day I heard a voice telling me in my spirit, "If you do not let the old go, the new will not come." That was the confirmation I needed to set out for Canada.

If you are reading this book and you are not religiously inclined, that is okay. Whatever its form, you need to find a confirmation for your conviction before taking a leap into the unknown.

The next challenge was convincing my loved ones to let me go, and then, of course, I had to raise the funds for my education and living expenses. I sold some possessions, liquidated some investments, and pulled funds from my savings to pay for tuition, living expenses, and my visa application.

Many people who have had to start all over will understand this situation and the feeling of doubt that can resurface. Even when you're convinced that you're making the right decision, you will still hear that small nagging voice that asks you how you're going to do it.

In my case, I had to move on my own first, without my wife and kids, to test the waters. This brought its own challenges, and if you're at a similar point in your journey, I see you. It was hard, but I was determined to make it irrespective of the many what-ifs. And I did!

Are you in a place where your what-ifs are drowning your convictions? I know that feeling. Let me say this gently: If you are waiting for everything to line up perfectly, you may never move. In my experience, things get figured out one after the other as you go.

In the days leading up to my departure, I was torn between excitement and anxiety. It was clear that I was going to be by myself for a while. At family gatherings, my relatives celebrated my new opportunity, but their joy was tinged with concerns.

"How will you manage life by yourself in a foreign country without your wife and children?" one of my older siblings asked.

"I hope I will weather the storm," I responded.

Those last days at home were bittersweet. My wife, a gentle yet strong woman, worked tirelessly to prepare everything for my journey. She packed my suitcases with homemade snacks and reminded me to pray and hold onto my values all through the journey. "It might be challenging, my love," she said one evening. "But I know you to be smart and very courageous. Remember why you're doing this."

My siblings, particularly one of my older brothers, Chief Ehi, struggled with the impending separation. "Who will support me with resolving routine family squabbles when they arise? God has blessed you with wisdom and patience to resolve conflicts and deal with issues amongst siblings and in our extended family. How are we going to take care of our aged mother now that you are leaving the shores of Nigeria?" He asked many questions.

I couldn't even bring myself to tell my mother I was traveling so far from her, probably for a long time. *What if the news breaks her*, I thought, *and causes her to suddenly fall ill? What if she does not survive until my return?* As her youngest son, I had become very close to my mom, and she is as fond of me as I am of her. I could not go a day without calling her, and I would use any available opportunity to travel to Uromi to check up on her. I just couldn't bring myself to hurt her like that, so I agreed with my younger sister, Faith, to trivialize my trip using the fact that my wife and children were still in Nigeria. We hoped that it would soften the impact and buy us some time to figure out how best to inform her of my big decision.

When I finally took off that fateful day in December, I felt a mixture of excitement and trepidation. At the airport, the weight of the moment hit me like a tidal wave. As I passed through the security checks, I turned to see my family waving. My wife's tear-streaked face and my children's solemn nods stayed with me as I boarded the plane. That was when the full weight of stepping into the unknown truly sank in.

"Life begins at the end of your comfort zone."
—NEALE DONALD WALSCH

The lights of Saint John Airport flashed like beacons of hope against the cold December night. I had been waiting for this moment for a long time. There had been a delay in the approval of my study permit due to a post-COVID backlog at Immigration, Refugees and Citizenship Canada (IRCC).

My brother-in-law, Taiwo Adejugbe, picked me up from the airport. The air was crisp and biting, far colder than anything I had ever experienced, even after previous travels to the United States of America, Dubai, and the UK. Still, the air carried the thrill of possibility and a better life.

My first impression of Canada, based on my research and planning, had been the sheer scale of everything: the sprawling highways, the towering skyscrapers, and the endless array of people rushing to destinations. However, this was not the case in Saint John, New Brunswick. The drive to the city offered a glimpse of calm and remoteness.

Saint John was especially quiet compared to my former home. Lagos is crammed with people, and the air there is alive with the hum of daily life: chatter on street corners, vendors selling their wares, and children playing in the streets. The city of Saint John felt small, still, and dauntingly remote to me. You will understand this feeling if you've had to move from a big, loud, and busy city to a smaller, quieter one.

Are you in a phase of your journey where it looks as if you have left something big for something smaller? I would say hold on. Do not give up yet. There is still so much to unpack. Do not be discouraged by the size. Have an open mind, and look out for the big things and opportunities within the small things.

With a warm welcome from Taiwo Adejugbe and his family, I unpacked my luggage and thought to myself, *this is a land of opportunities. With my experience and God's favor, I will certainly be successful.* I knew I would have to work hard and push boundaries to unlock the opportunities that awaited me, but I had no doubt there would be opportunities to prove myself and also learn in the process.

Permit me to pause here to say that when you are doing something new, what you tell yourself matters. Whether you are starting a new business, taking a new course, starting a new job, or starting a family, your mindset essentially drives your actions and conversations. If you believe you will make it, you will, but if you see only the negatives or obstacles and fill your mind with negatives, there is the chance that your progress will be impeded.

Within days of arriving, only recently recovered from jet lag and still in shock about the cold weather, I was thrust into the reality of balancing my studies and survival. I hadn't anticipated the depth of loneliness that would come with living abroad alone for a long time. Back in Lagos, I had been surrounded by people who knew me: family, neighbors, and friends who shared my culture, language, and humor. Here in Canada, I felt invisible.

Meals were particularly difficult. Sitting alone in my apartment and dealing with the pressure of making my meals between lectures, meetings, and other academic commitments, I often thought of family dinners where everyone would gather around the table, laughing and sharing stories. I tried cooking some of my favorite dishes from home, but they never tasted quite the same. As I became distracted by assignments, the food often got burned on the stove!

Video calls with my family became my lifeline. But while they brought comfort, they also deepened my yearning for home. Seeing my nephews and nieces grow and change without me, hearing the street sounds I had once taken for granted and now missed—it all left a hollow ache in my chest.

Canada differs significantly from my home country in sociocultural norms. Canada typically emphasizes individualism, punctuality, and personal space, while I was used to community, collectivism, and close interpersonal relationships. Communication in Canada is fairly indirect and polite, whereas in my home country, directness and expressive interactions are more common. Canada takes an egalitarian approach and has a flat social hierarchy: the use of first names to address even authority figures was surprising to me, as I was accustomed to a pronounced social hierarchy that values reverence for elders and authority by addressing them with titles. Canadians often prefer scheduled interactions where almost everything has to be pre-booked, including something as simple as opening a bank account, while I was used to a culture that embraced spontaneity.

It was Hofstede's cultural dimensions theory in practice. I was conscious of how these differences were going to affect my daily life, education, and relationships. As I made adjustments, I felt like a toddler learning to walk. If you are in this phase of your journey, you may feel out of place or inadequate, and that is normal. I was also tempted to feel that way. Be patient with yourself and the process. Be curious; seek knowledge and understanding of the meaning and history behind the cultural values. Be mindful of the fact that you are not the only one in the room, which means filtering your slang, gestures, tone, and actions. Lastly, practice the culture of your new environment. The more you practice, the more it becomes your second nature. Everything will become clearer as you progress in your journey with an open mind.

Despite my initial difficulties, I found solace in the belief that every challenge was a stepping stone to my dreams. I reminded myself that I was in transition and that I would soon graduate from my MBA program and pick up my career again. My upbringing in Nigeria taught me resilience and faith in God, and I leaned on those pillars to navigate the challenges of my new life.

Integrating into Canadian Society

Given everything I've shared, you will not be surprised to hear that I became curious about how to deliberately integrate into Canadian society and better understand the culture and sensitivities of my new environment. I took on a part-time job at Wendy's, working late into the night after long days filled with lectures and seminars. The shifts were grueling with long hours of standing, but the experience of interacting with locals and learning from them was a great compensation beyond the paycheck. I also worked part-time at The Brick (a retail store in Saint John) and at Compass Canada (a provider of hospitality services), where I met with locals and internationals from different strata of society. These experiences broadened my mind and equipped me with the practical knowledge and tools to navigate cultural sensitivities.

Over time, I started to find small pockets of belonging. I was pleasantly surprised to find students who shared my struggles. Pratik, a shy but kind student from India, and Chetan, an extrovert with a contagious laugh, quickly became my friends. We bonded over study sessions and group assignments. They shared stories of homesickness and cultural shock. With them, I felt that I was not alone in a way I hadn't before.

I also began exploring Saint John, discovering its rich cultural tapestry. City Market, with its vibrant mix of cuisines and eclectic shops, became a favorite spot. There, I found shops owned by locals who often chatted with me, offering warm smiles and a sense of community. If you feel lonely in a new environment, I'd recommend that you explore with an open mind. Connect with local community events, visit historical sites, and discover the beauty and richness of what your new environment has to offer.

Taiwo Adejugbe and his friend Adebayo Abiodun provided soft landing in every way possible. They guided me through essential steps of settling in. Taiwo assisted me to secure a safe apartment, assisted with furnishing it, and even supported me in buying a reliable student car. Their hands-on guidance extended to navigating daily life in a new country. Their support made my transition smoother, helping me avoid common mistakes and focus fully on settling down and succeeding academically from the very beginning.

Within the church community at RiverCross Church, I found a vital source of support. Members warmly welcomed me, helping me settle into my new environment. They helped me navigate public transportation and understand local customs. They also provided emotional support during times of homesickness. Rosalie and Reverend Steve McMullin became like my second family, inviting me and other newcomer students to their home for a Boxing Day dinner and ensuring that I got a free ride to and from church every Sunday.

Pastors Robert Nylen and Joe Page also created opportunities for students to connect with other students and with church members, fostering a sense of belonging and friendship. Pastor Rob would often check on me with a warm smile and ask, "How is the MBA program going? I know it's tough, but guess what? Others have made it through, and so will you." Those words meant more to me than he could have imagined.

Through weekly services, shared meals, and prayer meetings, I felt spiritually uplifted and embraced. Jan Cameron, the head of hospitality, showed kindness and gave hugs; her warmth eased my transition, making Canada feel like a second home despite the cultural differences. I was surrounded by very kind people who were willing to go out of their way to support my well-being. I later gave back by volunteering on the RiverCross transportation team, helping to drive newcomers to and from church.

At school, I began to excel in my MBA program, fueled by a relentless curiosity and drive to succeed. My professors and fellow students noticed, often commending my work ethic, innovative thinking, and thoughtful contributions in class. Dr. Mercy Oyet, one of my instructors, became a mentor to me, offering guidance and encouragement when the weight of study responsibilities felt unbearable. What endeared her to me was her patience and her willingness to listen to students as they described their challenges, which ranged from academic pressure to child minding, parking, snow, and networking, to name a few. Rarely have I met anyone with such patience and listening skills.

Chris Weir was another source of inspiration. Beyond being an excellent sales and business development instructor, he genuinely empathized with students and understood our struggles. On one occasion during his sales class, he said, "I know this is overwhelming; it is a lot to take in. I'd understand if you fall asleep on me, but I assure you that you will be all right. You have what it takes to go through your journey and excel." Those words were soothing to me and many other students.

If you're reading this book because you want to better understand and support an immigrant or newcomer, please know that your words matter. In their early months, especially, they need more grace and encouragement than you might realize.

Growth and Reflection

By the end of my second module or semester, I had transformed significantly. Challenges that had once felt insurmountable became opportunities for growth. I learned how to navigate the tough MBA program, contributed more to class discussions, and grew more self-assured. My part-time job at Wendy's, though exhausting, had enhanced my resilience and my appreciation for hard work as taught by my dad in my younger days.

But it was the intangible growth that mattered most. I developed a deeper sense of self-reliance and courage. I learned to embrace discomfort and see the unknown not as a threat but as a space for possibility.

That summer, I attended a community event at RiverCross Church. Surrounded by other newcomers, including international students, I reflected on my journey. I thought about the fears I had faced, the loneliness I had endured, and the friendships I had built. Every part of my experience, even the hard parts, was a blessing. From then on, I committed to continuously build my network in the Saint John community.

Are you at the point of your journey where you may be wondering whether you made the right decision in leaving your home and everything you had built? From one person who's been in this situation to another, I want you to know that it can and will get better.

Key Takeaways

1. **Do Your Research but Stay Flexible**

   Research your intended city and its schools, weather, transit options, and cost of living. Contact people already living in your new location and get firsthand insights. Having a solid plan in place will help ease anxiety. Nonetheless, things sometimes won't go as expected, so also prepare to adapt and learn as you go. What if the housing you arranged falls through? What if you find that the city isn't really where you want to be? That's why being flexible is key. It reduces the pressure and allows you to give yourself the grace to pivot when needed.

2. **Own Your Growth Journey**

   The unknown can be unpredictable, but it comes with opportunities to learn and grow. These experiences will shape you in ways you can't predict. Own your growth journey by being committed to continuous learning and development. Keep a journal about your wins and struggles, reflect often, and take pride in your growth. Be open-minded. Embrace challenges, especially those that stretch you beyond your limits, because they will help you grow toward the future you want to create. And remember to clap for yourself every step of the way! You deserve it!

3. **Believe in Yourself**

   Be confident in your ability to figure things out even if the path ahead isn't fully clear. Trust that the skills, experiences, and courage that brought you this far will carry you forward. Your downfall begins when you stop believing in yourself. Confidence doesn't mean having all the answers.

It means believing you can handle questions or situations as they arise. When you step into the unknown with self-belief, the unfamiliar becomes a place of amazing adventure, not fear. Have you ever heard that an individual with a will is unstoppable? Think about me! I fused sheer determination with positive energy, and boom—excellence and success by the grace and mercies of God!

4. Be Patient with Yourself

The apprehension of feeling out of place is normal when stepping into the unknown. However, giving yourself time to adjust is key. I'd say keep an open mind, and don't be afraid to ask questions or make mistakes because that's how you learn. I got confused and even frustrated many times, and at first, I was really hard on myself as I wondered why things weren't clicking into place. But I learned that patience is a great virtue. In many of those situations, I simply had to wait things out. If you are in that phase in your journey where nothing seems to be making sense, just be patient—everything will fall into place.

5. Budget and Spend Wisely

Financial stress is real when you're far from home, especially when you are self-sponsored. Track your expenses to make sure you are not spending more money than you have. Use credit cards wisely. Maxing out your credit cards repeatedly and not paying back on time impacts your credit score, and you do not want to live with the setbacks that come with a poor credit rating. Some retailers offer interest-free deferred payments; you may find it helpful to take advantage of those. Let your budget be centered around reasonable comfort and necessities rather than luxury until you have settled in fully.

To save money, familiarize yourself with the holidays when discounts and sales are typically offered, such as Black Friday sales, Independence Day, and Christmas holidays. Use coupons at the grocery store, and compare prices at different stores. Sign up for point plans when they are offered to help reduce your costs. And get familiar with thrift shops and part-time work rules. Every dollar counts!

Closing Reflection

Facing the unknown can be frightening, but it's also the place where the most significant growth takes place. It pushes you to believe in yourself, adapt, and find your hidden strengths. The rewards include greater resilience, new chances, and fresh viewpoints.

In the end, venturing into the unknown isn't just about what lies ahead. It's about discovering who you're becoming along the way.

The unknown isn't a void; it's a canvas and you are the brush.

CHAPTER TWO

Vision Casting—Painting the Picture of Your Ideal Life

"Create the highest, grandest vision possible for your life, because you become what you believe."
—OPRAH WINFREY

Many times, people move to a different location and then struggle to find themselves and live their ideal life. In most cases, this happens because we make important decisions without first setting a vision for what we want our lives to look like in our new environment. So, we move with the tide rather than acting with intention. We hear people are doing A, so we do A. All of a sudden, we hear it's B, so we switch to B. This is known as the "bandwagon effect."

That's why this chapter focuses on creating a personal vision for your life. As the saying goes: "If you can dream it, you can become it." What do you want your life to look like in your new environment?

I recall a conversation I had with a friend, Christian Ehizoba, during a business trip and vacation to the USA in 2018, long before I planned to move my family to Canada. As we drove through the streets of Sugar Land, Texas, he expressed concern about how some immigrants lose their way. He explained how easy it is for some people living in a new environment to get carried away by the excitement of the moment due to lack of a concrete plan to achieve their goals or the discipline to follow through with their plans.

Thinking back on that conversation takes me to the reasons I decided to relocate. As I thought of my journey and my new reality, I knew I needed to define my purpose—my "why"—and keep it clear in my mind. I wasn't carrying just my suitcases across the Sahara Desert and the Atlantic Ocean. I was carrying the dreams of my family, the hopes of my community, and the unshakable drive to get more out of life. Belief alone wasn't enough. It was clear that to truly build a life worth living, I needed a clear vision—a roadmap of sorts to guide me through the uncertainties and challenges of being a newcomer in a foreign land.

In my new environment, my vision became the compass that directed every step of my journey. It gave me clarity when I was overwhelmed, motivation when I was tired, and hope when the odds seemed stacked against me. It wasn't just about dreaming of success; it was about defining what success means to me and creating actionable steps to achieving it. As Stephen Covey wrote in his best-selling classic *The 7 Habits of Highly Effective People*, "Begin with the end in mind." That was what I needed to do.

If you are in the phase in your journey where you feel like you're drifting or unsure what your next steps should be, it might be time to pause. Step back and spend some time articulating your vision. It is not too late to create a mental picture of who you want to become. This critical exercise will help you avoid running in circles, getting easily distracted, or becoming frustrated.

To articulate your vision, create a personal vision statement. Scott Jeffrey writes: "A personal vision statement describes your future state—also called your Future Self. Think of it as your personal North Star." A vision statement is a forward-thinking statement that defines what's crucial to you and how you want to spend your limited time on Earth.

My personal vision statement is a combination of the values I want to live by, the contributions I hope to make, and the experiences I want to have. My personal vision is to live a life of poise and harmony, pursuing my passions while prioritizing my physical, emotional, and spiritual well-being.

Do you feel awkward about putting your vision into words? Does it sound too grand, as if your vision is too much to hope for? If so, let me introduce you to the newcomer's advantage.

The Newcomer's Advantage

As newcomers, we are starting with a blank slate in many ways because the life we left behind, although rich in culture, relationships, and experiences, is often far removed from the one we hope to create. That blank slate can be both daunting and liberating. For me, it meant I could dream freely without the weight of my past failures. I was no longer confined to the boundaries of the geographical location of Nigeria or limited by a feeling of being stuck in my career. Instead, I had the opportunity to redefine myself, to imagine a version of life that would combine the best of my roots with the opportunities of my new environment.

While some people wait until they arrive in their new location before thinking about their path, I spent time while still in Nigeria defining what my path would be and how I would achieve it. I knew I wanted to continue working in the energy sector. I researched energy companies in my intended location. I envisioned myself working as a project or operations manager—a goal that aligned with my previous professional experience and, more importantly, my passion.

But, as every newcomer knows, a new reality comes with challenges. The specifics are unique to each individual, but almost every immigrant faces the following challenges:

- **Cultural challenges** as we navigate unfamiliar norms and expectations.

- **Financial struggles** as we work to build financial stability from scratch.

- **Loneliness** because we are now far from family, friends, and our previous support systems.

- **Identity crises** as we try to reconcile who we were with who we want to become.

Facing such challenges can be difficult, but doing difficult things compels us to be resourceful, resilient, adaptive, and innovative. That is the newcomer's advantage. Because we are going through a trial by fire, we discover our true strengths, and that can translate into great strides in personal development and exceptional achievement.

I recall one evening in February 2023 when I had returned to my apartment after a busy day. I was feeling sandwiched between the pressures of academic commitments and the harsh winter weather. Sitting on my bed in utter frustration, I found myself questioning everything, just like the prodigal son (Luke 15:17). *Life was going well for me in Nigeria. Why did I not just stay there? How did I end up in this new and crushing reality?*

In that moment, I started to search for my "why." I began to ask myself crucial questions: Why did I leave Nigeria? What was the motivation? What did I set out to achieve? These questions helped me reflect on the vision that had brought me here. After about thirty minutes of deep reflection, I felt myself coming back all fired up to face any challenge. Knowing my "why" was motivating. I knew I wasn't going to give up on myself.

Are you in the middle of a new venture, such as a career change, business reorganization, or family relocation, and finding the weight unbearable? I completely understand, because I have been there. I believe that if you take a minute to reflect on your "why," you will get your groove back and rediscover the motivation to keep going. You cannot throw in the towel just yet.

But you can't rediscover something that was not there in the first place. This is where "vision casting" comes in. Personal vision casting is the process of crafting and communicating a clear, compelling picture of one's desired future, often in the context of career or personal development, to inspire and motivate oneself and potentially others to work towards achieving that vision.

So, the next question is the "how." I can imagine you asking, "How do I cast a vision? What should I do first?" Don't worry, I've got your back! Trust me; you are almost there.

Vision Casting: How to Do It

Below are the steps I followed in my vision casting. You can apply them to any situation to get your desired solution.

Step 1: Define Your "Why"

A strong sense of purpose is the cornerstone of any vision. Before you can clearly envision your ideal life, you must first ask yourself why you want it.

Part of my vision is to live a life of impact in the lives of others. My "why" for that vision includes my family, my neighbors, and my community. I feel more fulfilled when I not only put a smile on the face of another person but also help them maximize their potential and achieve their life dreams.

My background played a major role in shaping my "why." As a child, I saw firsthand how even the best skills can be rendered useless by lack of opportunities. I also witnessed my parents' commitment to provide the best for not just their children but others in our neighborhood and beyond. They touched many lives in many different ways, and their example inspires me in a profound way. I concluded that I wanted to do something significant not only for myself but also for my family and my community. I was determined to touch lives, just as my parents did.

My "why" also includes my faith. The Bible teaches that Jesus Christ came that we may have life and have it to the fullest (John 10:10). I wanted to live that full life Jesus spoke of. Anything short of that would mean settling for less. I knew I could have more out of life than I had achieved prior to relocating.

You may have a different "why." Your "why" could be your children, your broader family, your community, animals, the environment, your country, or all of humanity. Whatever your vision includes—financial stability, leaving a legacy, changing the world, or just living a happy and fulfilled life—your "why" must be strong enough to hold you steady during the inevitable storms. Give your motivations some thought. Put them in writing. Review them frequently. They are the vitality that will sustain your vision.

Step 2: Imagine Your Ideal Life

Vision casting requires imagination. Close your eyes and picture your life five, ten, or even twenty years from now. What does it look like?

For me, it started as a simple mental picture:

- I saw myself working in an energy and engineering firm, designing solutions and leading projects that made a difference in people's lives.

- I imagined owning a comfortable home, a place where my family could gather and feel at peace.

- I envisioned having vast resources—not wealth for wealth's sake, but the ability to support my loved ones and invest in causes I cared about.

- I saw myself speaking, writing, and publishing books about personal development to support people who are struggling with challenges I have experienced

- I dreamed of giving back by creating opportunities for others to achieve their dreams, just as I was working toward mine.

These images weren't just daydreams; they were vivid, detailed visions. I could see the office where I worked, the neighborhood where I lived, and even the conversations I had with the newcomers I would mentor. Because my vision was very detailed and clear, it felt real. This made the vision more motivating and effective in helping me define a path to reach my vision.

Here are a few practical exercises that may help you envision your ideal life:

1. **Write a letter to your future self.** Describe your life in vivid detail as if you're already living it. What are you doing? Who are you with? How do you feel?

2. **Create a vision board.** Use pictures, words, and symbols that represent your goals. Keep it somewhere you'll see it daily.

3. **Visualize daily.** Spend a few minutes each day imagining your future. Let that vision stir your emotions, and let those emotions sink in. They will keep you motivated.

Step 3: Set Clear Goals

A vision without goals is just a wish. To turn your vision into reality, you need to break it down into actionable steps.

When I started my journey, my goals were simple:

1. Complete my MBA program in one year with distinction.

2. Secure a project manager role in an energy company within one month of graduation.

3. Focus on cultural and economic adaptation by volunteering in two organizations relevant to my interests.

Each goal was specific, measurable, and time-bound. Having goals gave me a clear direction and a sense of progress, even when the bigger vision felt far away.

Here's how you can set goals for yourself:

- **Short-Term Goals (1–2 years):** Focus on immediate needs, such as finding a job, building a network, or improving your skills.

- **Medium-Term Goals (3–5 years):** Think about what's needed to achieve stability and growth such as career advancement, financial security, or personal development.

- **Long-Term Goals (10+ years):** Envision the legacy you want to create, whether it's building wealth, supporting your family, or making a broader impact.

Step 4: Build Your Support System

No one achieves success alone. Along the way, I realized the importance of surrounding myself with people who believed in my vision and were willing to support me. For me, that support came from mentors, peers, and community groups. My pastors and professors offered guidance when I felt exhausted by my academic workload. Fellow newcomers shared their experiences and advice, and my family and friends (such as "FOREVER KINGS") back home provided emotional support even from thousands of kilometers away. If you are a newcomer, seek out people who inspire you, challenge you, and encourage you to keep going.

I also reached out to others who had arrived before me. I visited both newcomers and locals to understand the peculiar dynamics of my new environment from their perspectives. I was determined to learn lessons that would be applicable to my journey.

One such person was Glen Fillmore, the vice president of strategic growth and transformation at Saint John Energy. I met him during my MBA Business Consulting Project (BCP) as I worked with his team at that time. I took every opportunity to tap his wealth of experience in strategic management and transformational leadership. His insights on leadership and workplace dynamics solidified my career plans and choices. He became my mentor and cheerleader from the first time I reached out. When I got my job at Irving Oil,

Glen set me up for career success by giving me access to his personal library. He also gifted me a book, *The First 90 Days: Proven Strategies for Getting Up to Speed Faster and Smarter* by Michael D. Watkins. I highly recommend this book to anyone starting a new job or role.

Another person who was a tremendous source of support for me was Heather Acker, cofounder of ConnexionWorks. She is an entrepreneur and an advocate for community and business development. I met Heather through my MBA program: I registered as a mentee in the UNBSJ-MBA mentorship program, and Heather was assigned as my mentor. She showed genuine kindness and interest in my career goals and aspirations. Her contagious smile, positive energy, and commitment to helping newcomers thrive were of immense benefit to me. She would often say to me, "I am always here. Whatever door you need opened, just let me know. If I don't have the key, I should know someone who does."

You need your own support system. Take time to find and nurture it. To build your support system, you can start with newcomer and settlement centres (YMCA, SJNC, etc.), get involved in community volunteering, join cultural or faith-based communities, connect through education and trainings, and find a mentor or accountability partner.

Step 5: Embrace Adaptability

One of the most important lessons I learned from vision casting is that life rarely goes according to plan. The vision you cast today may evolve as you grow. When I first envisioned my ideal life, I knew I had to be prepared for the twists and turns. "Nothing good comes easy," it's said. So, I was ready to adjust to changes in the environment but with my mind on the goal. Should you be struggling with twists and turns, be flexible. Allow your vision to adapt to new opportunities, challenges, and insights. What matters is staying true to your core values and purpose.

Step 6: Celebrate Small Wins

Building your ideal life is a marathon, not a sprint. Along the way, it's important to acknowledge and celebrate your progress, no matter how small.

For me, those moments included:

- Starting my first part-time job (at Wendy's, a fast-food restaurant).

- Receiving my first paycheck in Canada.

- Taking up a sales associate role in a retail store (The Brick Saint John).

- Landing my business consulting project at Saint John Energy.

- Landing my first permanent job in Canada.

- Returning to the UNBSJ MBA program as a guest speaker.

- Buying my first car in Canada.

- Buying my first house in Canada.

Each milestone reminded me that I was moving closer to my vision, and that gave me the motivation to keep going. Pause here to reflect on the milestones you've achieved. Celebrate them with the people around you, particularly those in your support network who are your biggest cheerleaders. Sometimes it is easy to focus on the struggles and forget to acknowledge one's own successes. Celebrating your wins reminds you that you are making progress. It's also a chance to practice gratitude for the lessons you've learned and the people who have helped you along the way. Those good feelings will keep you motivated and focused.

Key Takeaways

1. **Keep your vision simple, memorable, and focused.** A vision that is vague or overly complex won't inspire or guide action. You should be able to repeat it and see how your daily actions align with it.

2. **Paint the picture.** Use stories, metaphors, and vivid imagery to help you envision the future you're describing. The more tangible it feels, the easier it will be to pursue.

3. **Connect your vision to action.** A vision without a plan is just a dream. You have to understand and outline how the vision translates into practical steps and fits into daily priorities. Ask yourself regularly: *Are my actions supporting or sabotaging my vision?*

4. **Stay flexible.** Vision requires adaptability. Stay open to modifying your vision as circumstances change, without compromising your core purpose.

5. **Celebrate your wins**. Recognizing your progress fuels momentum. Focus on steady progress instead of perfection. In my public speaking engagements, I often highlight stories about achievements that reflect my vision and action. This keeps me motivated. Let your progress motivate you, too.

Closing Reflection

Vision casting is essential for inspiring and guiding ourselves and others toward a shared future. A strong vision motivates us to act and to persevere even in the face of challenges. But vision casting isn't just about achieving personal success; it's about creating a life of meaning and impact. As a newcomer, I've come to see my journey as part of a larger story—one that includes not just my own dreams but the dreams of those who may be inspired by my story. Today, my vision extends beyond my career and financial goals. It includes mentoring other newcomers and contributing to causes that matter to me. My success isn't just mine; it's a bridge for others to cross.

As you cast your own vision, ask yourself: How can my life make a difference? What legacy do I want to leave behind? Your journey may not be easy, but remember this: the challenges you face today are shaping the person you need to become to achieve your vision. Every step, no matter how small, brings you closer to the life you desire.

So, take that first step. Dream boldly, plan wisely, and never stop moving forward. Your ideal life is waiting for you to create it.

"Where there is no vision, the people perish."
—Proverbs 29:18

CHAPTER THREE

Time Management—The Key to Success as a Newcomer

"The bad news is time flies.
The good news is you're the pilot."
—MICHAEL ALTSHULER

Time is often described as a great equalizer; a resource distributed without bias or favoritism. But time can feel like an enemy when you are a newcomer. When you're juggling competing priorities such as academic success, career ambitions, cultural integration, and personal growth, time quickly becomes a relentless force. It can feel like a runaway train, threatening to derail professional and personal aspirations.

My first month in Canada was tough. Before I left Lagos, I thought that my academic workload might be heavy, as the UNBSJ MBA program was a two-year academic program compressed into one year, and I might also need to take some part-time job roles to defray minor bills while in school. What I didn't anticipate was the pace of life in my new environment. Activities that would have filled an entire day in Nigeria were compressed into a few hours in Canada. It felt as if there were not enough hours in the day. I also said yes to too many things, such as group projects, workshops, volunteer opportunities, and even impromptu coffee chats with classmates. My productivity plummeted as academic deadlines drew closer. I had come to pursue my dreams, yet it often felt like those dreams were pursuing me.

The Newcomer's Grind: A High-Stakes Balancing Act

Like many other newcomers, I brought more than physical belongings with me to Canada. I carried high standards and the unwavering determination to make my family and myself proud. This was a major reason why I was overcommitting myself. Moreover, even ordinary activities were more draining than before, as I was constantly having to navigate cultural differences, language nuances (such as subtle differences in meaning, tone, or style), and unfamiliar academic expectations. The loneliness of living away from my family amplified my stress and made it harder to concentrate on my studies.

The tipping point came when I almost missed the deadline for a critical assignment. That was my wake-up call. I knew that if I wasn't careful, this situation would repeat itself, and the next time could be disastrous. Something had to change. It was a tough moment, but it forced me to take a hard look at how I was managing (or failing to manage) my time.

Strategies that Worked for Me

I quickly understood that time management would not only turn the tide, it might also make the difference between failure and success. I needed not only better time management skills but a complete mindset shift. I started approaching my graduate studies as I would a strategic project with critical time constraints: with clear objectives, actionable plans, and constant evaluation.

If you're already doing this, bravo! If not, here are some strategies that helped me:

1. Prioritizing with an Eisenhower Matrix

I started by listing all my obligations and classifying them using an Eisenhower matrix—a tool that helps to prioritize tasks based on their urgency and significance. It's okay if you have never heard of this before; it is easy to learn and use.

To create an Eisenhower matrix, divide a page into four quadrants labeled as shown below. For each task on your todo list, ask yourself: Is it urgent? Is it important? Then list the task in the appropriate quadrant. Your completed matrix will make it clear which tasks you should prioritize.

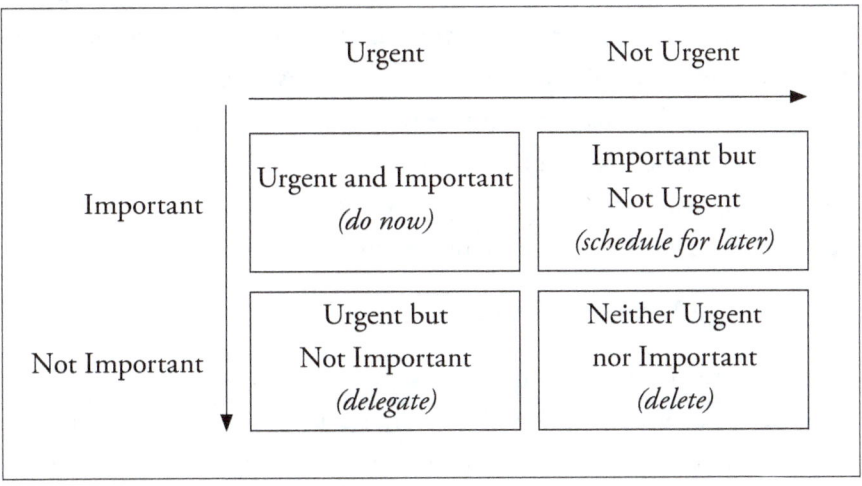

My Eisenhower matrix helped me divide my tasks up as follows:

- **Urgent and Important:** Assignments, lectures, immigration paperwork.

- **Important but Not Urgent:** Networking events, building friendships, self-care.

33

- **Urgent but Not Important:** Replying to less-important emails, attending less-important meetings.

- **Neither Urgent nor Important:** Scrolling endlessly on social media, binge-watching shows.

The Eisenhower matrix can help you focus on high-value activities while reducing unnecessary distractions, just as it did for me.

2. Learning How to Say No

Saying yes to everything was making it increasingly difficult to live up to my commitments, fueling my procrastination. So, I had to learn to say no, not just to others but to my own impulses. For example, I remember an occasion when I was racing to finish an assignment and I received a text message from a friend about a sale at the McAllister Mall. The sale was ending the same day my assignment was due. The limited window for taking advantage of the sale created a sense of urgency, but I realized that going to the sale was less important than meeting my assignment deadline. There would always be more sales, but I had only one chance to submit this assignment on time. So, I skipped the mall. I may have missed the opportunity to save some money in that moment, but I also got the score I needed to move to the next level in my academic pursuits. The takeaway: Not every opportunity deserves your attention. Focus on the ones that align with your vision.

3. Creating a Structured Routine

I began to structure each day like a project, breaking it into phases with each phase serving a purpose. This took a lot of discipline and determination, plus some self-awareness. I knew I was most effective in the early hours of the morning. So, I did activities that required critical thinking and deep focus during this time and moved less cognitively intense activities to later in the day. I remained flexible, because no two days are ever exactly the same. Still, creating a structure helped me to reduce stress by bringing clarity to my day, thereby eliminating wasted time caused by indecision. It also increased my productivity by helping me balance work, rest, and personal growth. Try a structured schedule to reduce decision fatigue and boost your productivity.

4. Leveraging Technology

I embraced technology tools to keep me on track. For example:

- **Google Calendar:** I scheduled everything from assignment deadlines to relaxation time.

- **Trello:** I created boards for my academic, personal, and work commitments, tracking progress and celebrating small wins.

- **Microsoft OneNote:** I used this for detailed notes and to-do lists, ensuring I never missed critical tasks.

These tools became my external brain, freeing up mental energy for deeper strategic thinking. If technology isn't your thing, that's okay. A traditional pen-and-paper planner works just as well for structuring your day as long as you commit to using it consistently.

5. Managing Time Zones and Family Connections

As a newcomer who had come without my family, I needed to maintain a constant connection with them. I had to create time daily to speak with family members, and the time zone difference made regular calls difficult. Those calls were what got me through those early days, but it was tough with a time zone difference of four hours or more. I would call my wife at least every other day. As the days went by, the struggle to balance calls from home with my immediate responsibilities intensified. I had to sit back, reflect, and prioritize. I realized that prioritizing being present in my new environment was essential for my immediate growth. I reduced the number of hours I allotted to calling Nigeria. I stopped trying to be everywhere at once, physically and emotionally. I learned to honor my limits so that I would not crash. If you are in a similar situation, believe me, I get it. You need to prioritize your time to avoid burnout.

Key Takeaways

1. Prioritize.

Try the Eisenhower Matrix, or look for books and videos on the subject of prioritizing tasks.

2. Learn to Say No.

Not every ask deserves a yes. Saying no respectfully sometimes is not a bad idea. Develop the habit of working within your limits to achieve maximum productivity.

3. Have a Daily Routine

Have a planned list of activities with allotted times in your day. Over time, small consistent actions build discipline and lead to lasting habits. Ultimately, a routine creates balance between productivity, rest, and personal growth.

4. Leverage Technology

Start by choosing simple, user-friendly tools like calendar apps or task managers that align with your workflow. Use them to set priorities, block out time for focused work, and set reminders for key deadlines. However, be careful not to get bogged down in technology at the expense of the bigger picture. Technology should support your goals, not become the goal.

5. Maintain Family Connections Wisely

Use video calls, messaging apps, and shared photo albums to stay emotionally present. Be mindful about balancing your family communication with your new responsibilities and opportunities in Canada. Prioritize quality over quantity. Meaningful conversations go further than constant updates.

Closing Reflections

This chapter is about time management, but it's also about self-management. I learned that effective time management isn't about squeezing more into every hour. It's about aligning your activities with your values and aspirations.

Time management is life management. If you can master your hours, you can master your future. To every newcomer, I dare to say that the clock is not your adversary; it is your silent partner, waiting for you to take control.

Yes, success is important, but so is your mental and emotional well-being. Success, they say, doesn't come from doing everything but from doing the right things at the right time.

"It is not enough to be industrious; so are the ants.
What are you industrious about?"
—HENRY DAVID THOREAU

CHAPTER FOUR

Stories of Resilience

*"Rock bottom became the solid foundation
on which I rebuilt my life."*
—J.K. ROWLING

More than just a buzzword, resilience is a vital life skill. It's our ability to adjust, endure, and flourish under trying conditions. Whether you're navigating academic demands, pursuing a career, adjusting to a new culture, or managing your financial obligations, you need to be resilient. Resilience applies to anyone and everyone. However, one of the most powerful ways to understand resilience is through the eyes of an international student.

In my case, there were days when challenging situations stared me in the face, daring me to give up. Let me talk about the day I returned home late in the evening, tired and battered by snow and hunger. It was a hectic day of jostling between classes and my part-time work. I had a group meeting that same night and a class presentation the following day. Everything felt so overwhelming. I had no family or friends around or any support in sight.

I started cooking dinner but fell asleep halfway through, only to be awakened by the smell of beans burning on the stove. Frustrated, I sank onto my bed. I could barely keep the tears from flowing. I had so many thoughts running through my mind. *How did I get myself in this bad situation? Why did I leave my family to study in Canada without support? How will I manage this journey all by myself? Should I just give up and return to Nigeria, where I still have thriving businesses and can easily get a stable job?* In that moment, I felt like giving up, pulling the plug on the whole endeavor, and turning back.

But in the middle of my disillusionment, frustration, and confusion, I paused. I reflected on the very reason for leaving and the goal I had set. *What if my children asked me later in life why I didn't succeed on this journey? Would I be able to sincerely say that I did all I could have or should have? Am I really at my wits' end, or could I try a little harder?* It felt too early to throw it all away.

Then and there, I made a decision: nothing would stop me from achieving my goal. I had to maintain my focus and vision and keep my eyes on the ball. Then hope stirred in my mind. I remembered the revelations I had experienced and my well-painted visions about my future. I remembered the scriptures and the prayers from my different fellowship groups and pastors. I cast my mind back to what was at stake.

I resolved not to give up, not just for my own sake but for the sake of others who looked up to me. I knew that one day my story would inspire my kids and others coming behind me. And there began my journey of resilience.

I have had the opportunity to interact with some other international students, and one thing I found we had in common is our resilience. So, let's pause my story for a moment to hear the stories of other international students who, like me, left behind all they had known for the promise of the unknown.

These are their stories of resilience.

Anonymous

When I moved to Canada as an international student and mother of a soon-to-be-teenage daughter, I knew it wouldn't be easy, but nothing prepared me for just how challenging it would be. My academic program was mega stressful. Financial stress was another: rent, groceries, my daughter's needs; we had to stretch every dollar impossibly far.

The weather was another shock. My experience of winter in other countries did not prepare me at all. It was a long and very cold season. I still recall waiting for the bus in freezing temperatures with frozen fingers and a weary heart, wondering how long I could keep going.

Balancing academics with parenting was also overwhelming. There were moments when I felt completely inadequate. While trying to keep up with assignments and late-night studies, I also had to be emotionally available for my daughter, who was silently carrying her own weight. She had to be strong while struggling to adjust to a completely new culture where social expectations felt somewhat foreign. The school system was different from what we knew back home—new teaching styles, not-so-familiar subjects, etc. At the same time, she was navigating the emotional rollercoaster of teenage life, such as making friends and finding her identity, in a place that was totally new. I remember walking into her room late one night and finding her in tears because she missed home. It broke my heart. Although I had assignments piling up, I knew at that moment that she needed me more. We leaned on each other, but ultimately, we leaned on God. I prayed with her, encouraged her, and watched as God gave her quiet strength beyond her years.

A job that suited my schedule and allowed me to support us came by grace and favor. God was my help. When I had no answers, He provided clarity. When I was emotionally and physically exhausted, His strength carried me. He surrounded us with meaningful friendships and connections, helpful class-mates, kind professors, wonderful pastors, community leaders, programs for newcomers, and even strangers who extended a hand at just the right time.

Looking back, I know it wasn't my strength that sustained us. It was God's grace, His provision, and His unfailing presence every step of the way.

Florence Olusope

In November 2022, I landed in Saint John with three kids, a grateful heart, and a head full of dreams. I came to pursue my MBA at the University of New Brunswick, but the journey quickly became about so much more—survival, courage, and resilience. My spouse remained back in Nigeria, and I found myself in a new world where I was parenting and studying alone. Housing was expensive, and even finding a suitable home was a challenge. Childcare for my three-year-old fell through repeatedly, leaving me to rely on last-minute favours that didn't always come through. I sometimes missed classes to stay home with the kids. I lost sleep. I doubted and questioned myself so many times.

The cost of living in Canada was sobering, especially when weighed against the exchange rate from my home country. I couldn't work part-time because the demands of school and motherhood were all-consuming. My days were long, and my resources, both emotional and financial, were stretched thin. Winter came with its unfamiliar snow and ice—I slipped and fell more times than I can count, including on Christmas Eve. But I got back up every time!

There were days I cried, nights I studied beside a sick child. But I kept going. I kept believing. Resilience, I've learned, isn't about having it all together. It's about moving forward even when the road is rough and lonely. It's in the quiet victories— submitting an assignment, making it through . . . one week at a time, smiling for your children, even when your heart aches.

This chapter of my life taught me that I'm braver than I ever knew. And today, looking back, I still can't believe I made it through. But it does get better. You just have to hang in there. So, hang in there!

Ashwinkumar Sankhwar

When I made the decision to move to Canada, I left behind not just my home but my family, my comfort zone, and a successful career in India's largest oil and gas company. I didn't have an MBA at the time, but I had over a decade of real-world experience, deep industry knowledge, and the motivation to build something greater.

I came to Saint John, New Brunswick, alone to pursue an MBA and broaden my horizons. Being away from my family while studying full-time was one of the hardest things I've ever done. The academic pressure, adjusting to a new culture, and navigating life in a new country without my support system—it pushed me beyond my limits, but it also shaped me.

After completing my MBA, I stepped into the Canadian job market with a fresh degree but no "Canadian experience." I had to start from the bottom again, proving myself one step at a time. I took every opportunity to learn, adapt, and showcase the value of my background.

Today, I work as a contract and procurement specialist for a Canadian oil refinery, bringing together my past experience and my Canadian education to contribute meaningfully to projects that matter. Best of all, I now share this life with my family, who joined me after my studies were completed.

To every newcomer starting over: Your story, your experience, and your resilience matter. The journey isn't easy, but if you stay focused and keep pushing forward, you'll find your place and your purpose here.

Samuel Olanrewaju Adeleke (Lariano)

Moving from Nigeria to Canada in pursuit of my MBA at the University of New Brunswick was a bold and life-changing decision. However, the journey was not without its challenges. One of the most immediate hurdles I faced was financial. Due to the steep depreciation of the Nigerian naira against foreign currencies, paying for tuition, accommodation, and daily expenses became a daunting task. This was compounded by the initial difficulty in securing a part-time job as I tried to navigate the Canadian job market and my academic workload simultaneously.

Adapting to Canada's cold climate was another significant adjustment, especially coming from a warm, tropical country. I also struggled with understanding the Canadian accent and communication style, which affected my confidence and ability to socialize or fully participate in class discussions. On top of all this, the emotional strain of being far from family, amplified by time zone differences, left me feeling isolated.

Despite these challenges, I found resilience through gradual adaptation and support. I reached out to International Student Services for guidance, found a peer group that offered encouragement, and started taking food orders and getting commission for deliveries using apps like Skip and DoorDash.

I learned to budget carefully and found creative ways to stretch every dollar. Over time, I adjusted to the weather, and I developed a routine that included staying connected with my family during overlapping hours. I also immersed myself in the local culture and practiced listening to Canadian English to improve my comprehension and confidence.

These experiences taught me perseverance, adaptability, and emotional strength. They shaped not just my academic journey but my personal growth and resilience.

Oluwadarasimi

There are moments in life that change you forever. Not in a loud, dramatic way, but in quiet, persistent ways that leave you stronger, wiser, and more deeply connected to who you are. This past year was filled with those moments for me. It was without a doubt the most challenging chapter of my life so far.

I made a decision that would stretch me to my limits: to leave my home, my comfort zone, and everything familiar behind, and move across the world with my nine-month-old baby for an MBA at the University of New Brunswick in Canada. It was a bold choice, one that seemed courageous on paper but often felt terrifying in real life. The journey itself was nothing short of epic. What was supposed to be a twenty-four-hour trip turned into something far more dramatic. We landed in St. John's, Newfoundland, instead of our intended destination of Saint

John, New Brunswick. Guess what? It was right in the middle of a hurricane. With barely any time to recover from the long flight, I had to brace myself for another eleven-hour journey, this time by road, navigating through unfamiliar terrain with a baby in my arms.

By the time we finally arrived in Saint John, I was physically drained and emotionally raw. But the challenges didn't stop there. Finding accommodation proved to be another uphill battle. The city was bursting with students, all vying for the few housing options available. I was running on fumes, carrying the weight of uncertainty, exhaustion, and responsibility. On some nights, the loneliness and pressure caught up with me. I remember walking through snowstorms after late-night classes, bundled up and weary, just to pick up my son. There were nights I cried myself to sleep, questioning everything. *Why did I choose this school? Was this all a mistake? Can I really do this?* The thought of deferring my studies, of returning to my home country and trying again another time, crossed my mind more than once. My husband, watching from afar, worried about us constantly. Yet through it all, he supported every choice I made. "Whatever you decide," he would say, "I'm with you."

But deep down, I knew I couldn't give up, not just yet. Even in my lowest moments, there was a flicker of something inside me. Call it determination, faith, or sheer stubbornness, but it kept me going. And my son, my beautiful little boy, became my anchor. He was with me in every class, every group meeting, every study session. We did it all together. I wasn't just pursuing a degree; I was building a life for both of us.

Somehow, one day at a time, we made it through. I completed my MBA at the University of New Brunswick—tired, yes, but proud. I walked across that graduation stage not just for me, but for every tear I shed, every night I doubted myself, and every moment I kept going when it would have been easier to stop. This phase of my life taught me that strength doesn't always roar. Sometimes, it whispers, "Just one more step." And so, to anyone who finds themselves on the edge of giving up, I say this: Don't! Keep going. The tunnel may be long and dark, but I promise, there is light on the other side. See you on the other side.

Jack

It was an exhausting cycle—submitting resumes, attending interviews, and receiving polite rejections or, worse, complete silence. Each rejection chipped away at the confidence I'd once had. My skills had improved. But, in the eyes of some Canadian employers, it was as though the experience I had acquired from my home country did not count. Instead of being celebrated for what I could bring to the table, I found myself constantly asked to prove that my past experience was relevant. But how do I prove that about something I've already done, but in a different place?

The frustration was palpable. How could I escape the feeling that my past was being erased, that everything I had achieved in my career no longer mattered because it didn't fit into the narrow mold that some Canadian employers were comfortable with? A job search isn't just about a job; it's about identity. It's about the years you've spent developing skills, learning lessons, and shaping your career. And yet, here you are, constantly having to start from scratch. The emotional toll was undeniable.

You may find yourself questioning: *Am I not good enough? What did I do wrong?* It may feel like the success you've worked for and the reputation you've built are somehow not valid anymore. This isn't just about a lack of Canadian experience; it's a sense of being "othered," being told that the skills you honed elsewhere somehow aren't as valuable as those developed in this new land.

For many internationals, the pressure is compounded by the need to support families and fulfill the dreams they cherish most. The frustration deepens when well-meaning people say things like, "You'll get there eventually, just keep applying." It's a message of hope, but sometimes it feels hollow, like you're constantly running in circles without getting closer to the finish line. You begin to wonder if that finish line will ever appear at all.

I refused to give up, I kept reminding myself that a job I must get! I kept attending networking sessions. I also consulted experienced HR practitioners to help improve my resume and help me with interview tips. Isaac was also very helpful through coaching and motivation as I navigated the difficult moments. I also kept praying and trusting God for help. Glad to say that I eventually got a job at one of the foremost banks in Canada.

Pratik Talajia

When I moved to Canada from India to pursue an MBA in project management at the University of New Brunswick, I faced numerous challenges that tested my resilience. Financial struggles were immediate. With limited savings and no job yet, I had to be frugal.

The weather was another unexpected hurdle. Coming from a tropical climate, I found the harsh winters daunting. I invested in proper winter clothing and learned to navigate icy roads. Over time, I adapted to the new climate, even finding joy in winter activities like ice skating.

While pursuing my MBA, I initially found it difficult to manage my part-time job and studies. At one point, I worked at

Boston Pizza as a cook, often having to walk home late at night because there were no buses available. Later, I started another job at Walmart as a customer service associate.

Balancing these responsibilities was challenging, especially since I was returning to school after twelve years of professional life. However, my friends provided immense support, helping me manage my time and succeed academically.

Emotionally, being away from family was tough, especially since I was very close to them. I felt isolated and homesick. Video calls helped a lot, allowing me to stay connected with my loved ones. Additionally, I made new friends who became my family away from home, providing emotional support and helping me feel less alone.

After completing my MBA, I secured a job as an area manager with UPS, which allowed me to achieve a stable life. My story is a testament to the resilience and determination of newcomers. Despite facing numerous challenges, I overcame them through perseverance, adaptability, and a positive mindset. I hope my journey will inspire others to remain hopeful and resilient in the face of adversity.

Moses Mogbolu (The Marketing Guru)

In September 2022, I made a life-altering decision to resign from my flourishing job as product group manager at Vitafoam Nigeria Plc to pursue an MBA at the University of New Brunswick, Saint John. Just weeks prior, I had been named Nigeria's Outstanding Marketing Personality, a reflection of my dedication, creativity, and leadership in marketing. With a fulfilling career, corporate recognition, a brand-new car with a personal driver, and a loving family (my beautiful wife and four brilliant sons), life was comfortable. Yet, I chose growth over comfort and purpose over predictability.

Arriving in Canada with nothing but determination and my GTBank Dollar Card, I faced immediate uncertainty. My apartment wasn't available until October 1, 2022, but a single call to the pastor of RCCG Pavilion of Redemption secured temporary church accommodation for eight days. On my second day, Hurricane Fiona struck—my first real encounter with extreme weather conditions. Even Google Maps said it was "confused." It made me question: Did I make the right decision?

Despite the solitude and sleepless nights managing schoolwork, digital marketing clients in Nigeria, virtual conference speaking engagements, and 3:00-a.m. prayers with my family, I pressed on. I worked as a part-time customer experience associate at Walmart and H&M Group to immerse myself in Canadian work culture. I actively participated in networking events, community volunteer activities, and marketing forums, sharing insights and uplifting others. Helping others became my source of joy, even amid my own challenges.

After five months apart, I brought my family to Canada. Although neither my wife nor I had permanent jobs, we lived on my personal savings and faith. My business consulting project with Commissionaires New Brunswick and Prince Edward Island earned me commendation and awards, so I was very hopeful that I could secure a permanent job with them. However, I was ineligible for full-time employment due to citizenship restrictions—a humbling reminder of the hurdles immigrants face. Yet, I maintained close ties with the leadership and remained optimistic. After completing my module 5, I undertook a search for jobs that aligned with my career aspirations and professional experience. I set a target to submit a minimum of two applications every day. I got invitations to many interviews, but I mostly got rejection emails or the silent treatment from recruiters. I currently work as an assistant category manager at Kent Building Supplies. Although the recruitment process included over six different stages of assessment, I would say it was fast and smooth.

Three Powerful Lessons for Newcomers to Canada

1. **Adapt quickly.** Be willing to start small, embrace change, and keep learning. The faster you adapt, the quicker you will thrive.

2. **Stay visible.** Your network is your net worth. Show up, build relationships, and demonstrate your value consistently.

3. **Give to grow.** Helping others opens doors you never expected. Generosity is a multiplier of success.

Resilience isn't just about surviving. It's about evolving, rising, and thriving in the face of uncertainty.

Mutiat Adeleke

I'm sharing my story with the hope that it reaches someone who may be wondering if it's too late to start over or follow a new path.

I'm a wife and mother of four. I began my professional career in Nigeria in 2001 as a banker, and for many years I had a fulfilling career. I worked with great people and earned well. But by 2018, I started to feel a nudge—it was time to move on, even though I wasn't sure what was next. Should I start a business? Go into teaching? I explored both. I almost launched a "bottled water" manufacturing business, but the space I intended to rent didn't work out. I also enrolled in a teacher training program and paid the full tuition, but I had to drop out. The demands of the program didn't align with the reality of working full-time in banking operations—often seven days a week.

At that point, I had never seriously considered relocating abroad. My international experience was limited to vacations; living outside Nigeria just wasn't on my radar. But when I started learning about the Canadian immigration programs, something shifted. I began to research, and slowly, the idea grew. It felt like a place where my family could thrive. Still, the process looked long and complicated. And it was.

Choosing between the entrepreneurial route and studying was a challenge. I've always been hard-working and focused, but the idea of going back to school—especially outside my home country—felt daunting. It wasn't about the studying itself; I've always done well academically. The challenge was leaving behind my structured life, support system, and comfort zone.

Eventually, my spouse and I decided that, for the future we wanted, I would go back to school in Canada. I began with World Education Services (WES) credential evaluation. That alone took over a year, as my university department in Nigeria hadn't digitized its records. It felt like squeezing an elephant through the eye of a needle just to get my transcript.

After that came the struggle for admission. I was initially accepted at the University of Vancouver, but by the time the admission came through, the tuition had increased significantly. I looked elsewhere, found a better fit, and got in. Then came the study permit process—denied once before it was finally approved. The approval came in November 2021, which was too late for the Fall intake, so I had to defer to 2022.

I completed my studies in 2023 and started my current role as a project coordinator just a week after graduation. Life here in

Canada is very different from what I had before, but it's given me space to grow, especially in building relationships.

Now, I look back and ask myself: was it worth starting over in a new country at a stage of life when most people expect stability? Yes, it's been absolutely worth it.

So, here's my message to anyone who may be doubting themselves: don't let age, fear, or setbacks stop you from pursuing your dream. Even if the road is long, it's never too late.

John Olajugba

When the world slowed to a crawl in 2020, I sped up. COVID-19 had most people retreating into uncertainty, but for me it was a strange kind of liberation. I resigned from my nine-to-five with barely a second thought. My agribusiness was booming; I had over a hundred employees, and I was juggling it all while pursuing my master's degree at Covenant University, Nigeria's academic crown jewel. On the surface, it looked like success. But inside, something was off.

There was a vacuum, an itch I could not scratch. Maybe it was the suffocating atmosphere of the country, like the sky had ceilings, or maybe it was the feeling that I was meant for more than the bounds of my geography. I always knew I wanted to become a professor—not just any professor, but one with a global footprint, a voice in meaningful conversations, someone who could move the needle in society. And for that, I needed a PhD, preferably in North America. Thankfully, books and exams have always been my comfort zone. I aced my coursework at Covenant with distinction. Scored in the top percentile on the GRE without breaking a sweat. But the journey from dream to departure was anything but smooth. I applied for an

MBA at the University of New Brunswick, and when I got in, I thought, "Great, we are halfway there." But then the Canadian immigration gods decided to play a little prank. My study permit took nine whole months. Nine. I even started my MBA remotely from Nigeria, navigating time zones, power outages, and occasional cockroach sightings during Zoom presentations.

Then came my birthday. The morning started like any other until an email from IRCC landed in my inbox: *Your study permit has been approved.* I screamed. No, actually, I roared. That was the best birthday gift of my adult life. I called my parents, told a few friends, booked a December flight, and started counting down the days. Months melted into weeks, weeks into days, and suddenly, I was stuffing my entire life into two suitcases.

Leaving wasn't easy. My business. My family. My food, oh, my food. And let's not even talk about Nigerian suya, which I suspected I would miss more than some people. As we stood at the airport, my parents, siblings, and friends hugging me tightly, reality hit like a delayed punch: I was really doing this. I was walking away from everything familiar for a future wrapped in uncertainty. When I reached Nigerian immigration, something inside me cracked. I wept. Not the cool, cinematic kind of tears. No, this was shoulder-shaking, nose-dripping ugly crying. A man behind me muttered, "Isn't this the golden ticket everyone wants? Why is he crying like they just cancelled Christmas?" Good question! I did not know if it was grief, fear, or the question that kept haunting me: What if I fail?

I landed in Montreal dazed and numb, collected my study permit, and boarded my next flight to Saint John, New Brunswick. As the plane descended, I peered out the window, expecting the bright lights of a Canadian city. What I saw looked like a retirement village with snow: grey, quiet, and secluded. I remember thinking, "Wait, is this the Canada everyone's been shouting about?" Saint John was not what I expected. But there was no turning back now. With a few days to spare before classes began, I did what any determined newcomer would do: hit the job market. Full of hope, dressed in the only winter-appropriate coat I owned, I opened my laptop and applied for over a hundred jobs in a week. No calls. No emails. Just crickets. I was not naïve; I knew it would not be easy. But nothing prepared me for how invisible you could feel in a place so far from home.

Desperate, I reached out to the local Nigerian community. One guy said, "Bro, you need to change your name to John Smith if you want callbacks." We laughed, but the truth in his joke stung. Eventually, someone connected me to an employment counselor, a kind woman who took one look at my Nigerian-style résumé and said, "Well . . . this is a beautiful autobiography, but let's make it Canadian." We tore it apart and rebuilt it from scratch. I started attending job fairs, handing out résumés like flyers for a party no one wanted to attend. Three months passed. Nothing.

Then one snowy Tuesday—in Saint John, there are only two seasons, snow and pre-snow—I got a call from a retail store. Part-time. Minimum wage. Did I want it? Absolutely! That job paid my bills and gave me structure. It also gave me a front-row seat to Canadian culture: the obsession with weather apps, the addiction to Tim Hortons, and the way *sorry* could mean anything from "Excuse me" to "You're standing too close" to "You just stepped on my foot, but it is okay because I am Canadian."

Meanwhile, the MBA program at UNB was intense, a firehose of case studies, group projects, and back-to-back deadlines. But I was built for this. I leaned in, made friends from around the world, joined study groups, and spoke up in class even when my accent turned heads. I finished strong—with distinction again. Most of my classmates settled in Saint John after graduation. It made sense because the path to permanent residency in New

Brunswick was smoother, and the cost of living was bearable. But my compass pointed elsewhere. My dream was still alive: the PhD. And the acceptance letter had come from York University, Ontario. Fully funded. But with that opportunity came a paradox. New Brunswick offered me security. Ontario offered me purpose. "Are you mad?" one of my friends asked. "You are leaving Permanent Resident (PR) on a platter for more stress?" Probably. But I had faith, not the kind you tweet but the kind you pack into your suitcase when you move provinces with no backup plan. I told myself, "I did not come this far just to settle. I came to rise."

So, I left Saint John behind, again packing my life into suitcases. Ontario was faster, louder, colder in attitude, and ten times more expensive. But within weeks of arriving, I got nominated for permanent residency under the Federal Skilled Worker Program. Months later, I got an approval email that felt like a seal of destiny.

I am currently a PhD student at York. I have secured external scholarships. My research on social class and organizations is not just academic; it is personal. I have lived the class divide. I have climbed it, stumbled on it, and questioned it. And now I want to help dismantle the rigid ladders we have built in workplaces so that people do not have to be born into advantage to rise. That feeling of "vacuum" I once had back in Nigeria? It's finally getting filled, not by achievement but by alignment. It feels like I am no longer just chasing success. I am building meaning. And I am not done yet.

If you are reading this as a newcomer to Canada, perhaps freshly landed, overwhelmed, clutching your coat tight against a wind you weren't built for, I see you. I have lived the contradictions: joy and grief at the airport; purpose and doubt on the same pillow. I have submitted hundreds of resumes and received nothing but silence. I have worked jobs that didn't reflect my education just to pay rent. I have entered the wrong trains to the opposite direction. I have stood in unfamiliar cities wondering if I had made the biggest mistake of my life. I have questioned my decisions, too. But here is what I know now: Starting over does not mean starting from zero. It means starting from experience, just in a new place, in a new system, with a new language of success to learn.

Canada does not always open its doors easily. But it is a country that rewards persistence, adaptation, and purpose. It may take time for your qualifications to be seen, your voice to be heard, or your worth to be acknowledged. Do not let that delay convince you that you have made the wrong move. Some of us are not just immigrants; we are builders of bridges. Between cultures. Between classes. Between what is and what could be. My story is not unique because I succeeded. It is a spotlight on what so many of us do every day: persevere, pivot, and push forward. Whether you are chasing a degree, rebuilding a career, or simply searching for peace, you belong in the narrative, too.

So, carry your accent with pride. Carry your story like an armor. When it gets hard, which it will, remember this:

Nigeria made me, but Canada refined me.

Lessons Learned

Through each of the stories above, one key theme stands out: resilience! These stories illustrate how resilience helps newcomers adapt and thrive, transforming obstacles into milestones. Following are lessons I have learned about resilience.

1. Failure Is Not the End

Resilience teaches us that setbacks are part of the process. Failing doesn't mean that you're finished. It just means that you have learned a new way that didn't work at that time. It means a new opportunity has been opened to explore other possibilities. When something doesn't work out, pause and ask: *What did I learn from this? What can I try differently?* Every failure can be a stepping stone to success. Remember Jack's story? He failed to secure a job offer multiple times, but he did not give up. Instead, he kept evaluating his actions and inactions and tried to do things differently. Is this your experience as a newcomer? It could become very tempting to see the setbacks as the end of your journey, but learn from Jack. Look beyond the failure with a resolve not to give up and to continuously look for new ways to do things to get to your desired end.

2. Mindset Matters

The way you think impacts how you handle challenges. A growth mindset empowered me to view challenges as opportunities for growth. In the words of J. K. Rowling, "Rock bottom became the solid foundation on which I rebuilt my life." A person must develop a growth mindset, seeing problems as opportunities for growth rather than as obstacles to avoid. Have you paid attention to your inner voice/critic? Sometimes you hear, "I can't do this." You've got to challenge that voice with: "What if I can figure this out?" Remind yourself of the challenges you have overcome previously. Remember the situations you survived in the past. You can do it again. You are a hero! You can draw inspiration from Oluwadarasimi's story, where she said, "Even in my lowest moments, there was a flicker of something inside me. Call it determination, faith, or sheer stubbornness, but it kept me going." That is the right mindset to succeed.

3. Strength Comes from Struggle

Resilience isn't about avoiding pain; it's about enduring it and growing stronger. Hard times reveal inner strength that you might not have known you had. Allow yourself to feel the hard-hitting emotions without judgment. It's okay to not be okay. Practice positive self-talk. Focus on your strengths and successes rather than weaknesses and failures. As Florence said in her story, strength came from her struggles in looking after three kids while pursuing her MBA.

4. Support Systems Are Powerful

Being resilient doesn't mean doing it all alone. Asking for help, leaning on loved ones, and seeking guidance can make you stronger. I made a list of people I could text or call when I felt overwhelmed. Even a simple "Can we talk?" or "I need a distraction" can open the door to support. I've learned that resilience grows when we share experiences, support one another, and celebrate each step forward. It is said that vulnerability is universal. I recognized when I needed additional support and reached out to trusted friends, family, community, or professionals for help. My dear friend Amoge Ogu was very supportive when I felt overwhelmed in my journey. She was my coursemate, dependable friend, and ally. Her words of encouragement in some dark seasons were more than soothing. We had long conversations trying to figure out together how to keep going. In Lariano's story above, he built resilience by reaching out to the support system he had built. If you are a newcomer navigating your journey, resist the temptation to isolate yourself when facing challenges. Speak up to trusted supports and use available government resources to get the help you need.

5. Adapt and Overcome

Change is constant, and resilience helps us adapt to it. Whether you are facing a personal loss, a career shift, or any other unexpected life event, resilience gives you the tools to bounce back and keep moving forward. To avoid becoming overwhelmed, adaptability is key. When you find it impossible to achieve a goal in one way, you can adapt or pivot to a different way to achieve the same goal. Pratik, for example, wrote in his story, "I adapted to the new climate, even finding joy in winter activities like ice skating."

6. Set Realistic Goals

Setting realistic goals is important because an unrealistic goal has little chance of being met. To ensure a realistic path toward your goal, break it down into manageable steps. This gives you a clear sense of direction and progress, which will boost your confidence even in tough times. Celebrating each of these successes along the way will convince you of your ability to cope, adapt, and keep moving forward. Acknowledge every step forward, no matter how small. Reward yourself for consistency, not perfection.

Closing Reflection

Resilience is a transformative skill for newcomers if you truly desire to be successful. It enables adaptation to new environments, helping you overcome challenges and seize opportunities. By cultivating resilience through real-life experiences, building support systems, and leveraging available resources, you can turn challenges and setbacks into stepping stones for personal and professional success.

Are you embarking on a new journey or in the middle of a challenge? Remember that resilience is not about avoiding difficulties but about facing them with courage and determination. Your stories, challenges, and triumphs will shape you into a stronger, more capable individual, ready to excel in the world's dynamic landscape.

"Our greatest glory is not in never falling, but in rising every time we fall."
—Oliver Goldsmith

CHAPTER FIVE

Family, Children, and Culture Shock

"At first, I thought I was lost. Then I realized I was simply not where I was used to being."
—Unknown

Upon arrival in Canada, I found myself battling culture shock even though I had previously lived or visited other countries, including the United Kingdom, the United States of America, Dubai, and Gabon. Should I say the culture shock was different or deeper this time in Canada? Maybe so.

Canada comes with its own set of rules and rhythms. A strict sense of politeness dictates holding doors for others and speaking in soft tones. Pedestrians cross the street at designated points; drivers generally keep to speed limits; gas pumps are self-service. Access to fountain drinks is unlimited in some restaurants. (I felt like drinking them endlessly). Some stores allow you to return items and get your money back. Public school students don't wear school uniforms. The list of customs that were new to me is endless.

You know you're in culture shock when a simple trip to the grocery store feels like an adventure because most of what's on the shelf is unfamiliar.

Then came the exciting news that my family's visas had been approved, and they were set to join me after we had been apart for more than six months. I was excited about the reunion, but I was more concerned about how they would adapt to this new life. They would be navigating a new climate, making new friends, experiencing a new school system, and learning new ways of doing just about everything. I was particularly worried for my kids. How do you explain to your children that everything they've always known is about to change? How do you teach them that people can do the same thing in completely different ways and that neither is necessarily wrong? How do you help them process the identity crises lurking around every corner when you're still navigating your own?

The Canadian and Nigerian cultures are in many ways almost directly opposite each other.

As I battled these questions ahead of my family's arrival, I tried to engage their minds with a few tips on what they should expect in their first few days. I made video calls and showed them snowbanks, quiet roads, and slow-moving vehicles to help them prepare for their new environment. They were used to the loud and busy streets of Lagos and being surrounded by a large family. They were used to going to the beautiful beaches and playgrounds with their cousins. All of that was about to change in a couple of weeks, and every day that passed increased my anxiety and worry.

To worsen the situation, I recalled a conversation I had with one of my friends during a visit to the USA. He spoke about many immigrant families in the US whose children suddenly became rebellious after they started to socialize with other kids in their new environment. He also mentioned that some immigrant kids struggling with culture shock become depressed and anxious, leading to identity crises, low self-esteem, and poor grades in school.

Having lived in the UK myself, I had seen newcomers' families torn apart by divorce. While some believe that it could be their inability to manage the culture shock, others believe that financial stress fuels divorces abroad.

With these thoughts weighing heavily on my mind, I asked myself: How do I prevent my family from suffering the same fate? What would be the value of all the sacrifices of relocation—the hard work, the money spent, the mixed feelings of missing home every day—if my family doesn't survive the transition in one piece? Everything would be useless without my family intact.

Raising a Family Amid Crises of Adaptation

As the time of their arrival drew near, I spent more time praying and learning about what their biggest challenges might be. I had learned a few North American social norms, customs and traditions, and I thought, *Okay; I can begin with the known*, but there were also things I didn't yet know. So, I reached out to a few friends who arrived in Canada before me and had children around the same ages as mine. I wanted to see if there was something I could learn from their experiences.

The D-day came on June 7, 2023, when my family arrived to join me in Canada. It was time to face my fears and help them navigate their shocks. Here are some of our experiences.

School

The first shock we faced came from the school system. In Nigeria, kids could start elementary school as early as four or five years old, especially in private schools. In Canada, grade assignments are based on the child's age. This meant that my children, who attended private schools in Nigeria, were two classes ahead of their age when they arrived in Canada. We submitted relevant documentation to show their progress in the hope they could retain their current grades, but they were still moved back two grade levels. We wrote emails and attended several in-person meetings, all to no avail. So, we were left with the difficult task of explaining to our children why they had to repeat grades, and what that would mean for their academic and career pursuits.

As if that was not tough enough, they all woke up one day and said they didn't want to go to school. They complained that school was too boring. There were no tests, no assignments, and no motivation, especially as they had done this academic work two years prior. So, they were scribbling and coloring during class (funny how that works). Just when we thought things couldn't get worse, we began receiving calls from the school principal and the homeroom teacher complaining that our kids were too active in class and would not give others a turn to answer a question. We were getting calls like this about once a week. It was as chaotic for our three brilliant and amazing kids as it was for us.

Lack of a Support System

Back in Lagos, Nigeria, we were used to multiple support systems ranging from paid staff (like drivers, housekeepers, and security guards) to family members, including grannies and cousins who came around the house from time to time. These people didn't just provide the warmth of family and trusted allies; they also supported us in raising the kids. Things were different in Canada. We had no driver, which meant we had to drive ourselves and the kids everywhere we wanted to go. We had no housekeepers, which meant that every single chore, from cleaning to grocery shopping, fell to us. There were no cousins, aunts, uncles, or any other family members. It was more than culture shock; it was a whole new world.

One time, my son asked why we had no one to help us out with anything. Such help was something our children had been used to. Their world was changing, and fast. We needed proper strategies to support them in navigating this new terrain. Unfortunately, these aren't struggles that people talk about often.

Addressing Elders and Seniors

Another culture shock we encountered was how elders and seniors are addressed. In Nigeria, seniors are highly respected and hold positions of authority within the family and community. We see them as the custodians of wisdom, tradition, and knowledge. Addressing elders with deference and reverence is deeply ingrained in our upbringing. Our kids have been taught to respect and honor elders. Nigerians address seniors with terms that denote respect, such as Auntie, Uncle, Sir, Mr., and more formal titles like Grandfather and Grandmother—even when they are not our biological relatives. Nigerians kneel, genuflect, prostrate, or bow when greeting an elder. Anything less would be considered disrespectful and rude. In fact, looking an elder in the eye is unthinkable.

Canada, on the other hand, is a bit different. Seniors are often called by their first names. There is no kneeling or bowing, which to the average Nigerian means no honor. It was going to be tough to switch from the African context to the Canadian context. And back to the kids: how were we going to explain that what we had always taught them was suddenly not going to be true anymore? I had to find a creative way to explain that cultural differences do not mean that one culture is bad and the other is good.

Public Behavior Standards

When I landed in Canada, I was shocked to see that public smoking and vaping are a social norm among adults and teenagers. Revealing summer outfits and public display of affection were another set of concerns. We weren't exposed to these things in our home country, and while we respect individuals' right to make their own decisions, we wondered how far we would allow our children to stray from the norms we had grown up with.

Changing the Narrative: Strategies that Worked

Moving from one place to another means you will see cultures that are alien to you and challenge some of the values you hold dear. So how can we navigate these complex sensitivities? What do we need to do to raise morally upright, responsible, and godly children in our new environment? As a Christian, I had made a solemn promise to God not to be a part of any negative statistics, and so I came up with some strategies that have helped my family and I believe will help yours, too:

1. Be Intentional and Strategic

Many parents, upon relocating with children, struggle at first to make ends meet. This often means that we're not present for our kids, and we miss opportunities to reinforce our values and morals. Do I blame parents for working to put food on the table? Of course not; children need food to live and grow. The challenge is in knowing where to strike the balance between child-care and economic striving. The kids must not feel neglected. We have to learn how to prioritize and balance competing priorities.

What does priority mean in this context? Which should come first? Does anyone really have to come first, or should we just continue to adapt as we go? The thought trigger for me is this: what is the value of the riches or wealth if you have made money but come home to a raped child or a drug addict because you were not available to care and protect?

I decided to be strategic by leading the way with relevant conversations based on our family values and expectations. I prepared a deck of nineteen slides to drive the discussions in the family. Over two hours, with a few breaks, we talked about the realities of our new environment and the different changes to expect. We started with understanding our reason for moving abroad. Why had we left the luxury and warmth of family support to come to Canada? As the saying goes, abuse is inevitable if the reason for a thing is not known. Then we moved on to our family's core values, including honesty, courage, resilience, empathy, positive mindset, hard/smart work, and building strong relationships. Next was the topic of maximizing opportunities available through education, sports, leadership, and volunteering. Then we discussed lifestyle and agreed on a concise statement of our family's guiding principles.

A few things we emphasized to our children in this conversation:

- We told them there is no limit to what they can be under God in this new environment, and that they should not allow their skin colour, accent, body shape, or anything else stand in their way. Philippians 4:13 came in handy: "I can do all things through Christ who strengthens me." Through Christ, you can become anything.

- We told them we would be their biggest fans and support them in anything they chose to do. We committed to loving and caring for them in all situations as we navigated this new reality together.

- We sensitized them on how to speak up and stand up against bullies and other unpleasant situations.

- We informed our children that they would encounter many people whose beliefs, lifestyle, or disposition is different from theirs. We told them they must not disrespect or judge anyone, because those people have the right to be whatever they want to be.

- We told our children that they, too, have the right to their own beliefs and lifestyle, and that the rights of others do not preclude this.

We concluded that we must stick together as a family, uphold our Christian principles and values, respect others, and have open conversations. The goal of this session was to build a foundation in our children's minds against which to reference the realities they would come across as they grow in Canada. We ended with the following family nuggets:

FAMILY NUGGETS

I Can Do All Things Through Christ (Philippians 4:13)
Do Not Join a Multitude to Do Evil (Exodus 23:2)
I Will Not Trade Family for Anything: All for One, One for All
A Little Sleep, A Little Slumber . . . (Proverbs 6:10–11)

---

2. Plan Support Systems for Emotional and Mental Health

Homesickness is real! Our children missed their cousins, schoolmates, grandparents, and neighbors. My wife and I missed our parents and all the support systems we had built back home. So, the first thing we did was validate our feelings. We let the kids know that it is normal to miss home, and that it's okay to feel sad or anxious about being away from their familiar surroundings. Offering empathy helped our children feel understood and less isolated in their experience. Next, we encouraged them to look at the photos we brought along with us from Nigeria (including Granny's photos). These photos and other familiar items kept family and friends close to mind and helped us all feel their love and support despite the distance. Another effective way to manage homesickness was by maintaining communication. We made regular phone and video calls to stay connected with family members. These calls helped us feel more at ease and provided emotional support during times of discomfort.

3. Values and Identity Formation

We intentionally taught our children about the importance of preserving their cultural heritage while adapting to the new environment. We overheard our children talking to each other about their struggle with the temptation to think that their cultural and family values and identity were inferior to what they were seeing in their new environment. So, we came up with ways to help them make space for both cultures in their routines. We wore African prints and celebrated Nigerian holidays, and we also supported them as they participated in activities in their new school and community. We encouraged our children to feel proud of both their cultural background and their new experiences, building their self-esteem by embracing both cultures. It was important to us to emphasize our family values of honesty, empathy, hard/ smart work, courage, respect, positive mindset, resilience, and community. We continuously reminded them of their identity as Christians, as Africans, and as valuable members of their new community.

4. Understanding Diversity

Now that we were raising our children in a country as culturally diverse as Canada, we considered it essential to teach them about diversity and foster a sense of respect for all cultures. We highlighted the various customs visible in our new community. We had to model inclusive behavior by being respectful and open-minded toward others regardless of their race, ethnicity, gender, sexual orientation, abilities, or background. We encouraged our children to ask questions about differences they noticed, and we responded openly and honestly. This was crucial for creating a safe space where our children could feel comfortable talking about diversity. We used age-appropriate language and examples to explain differences in race, gender, culture, language, religion, family structures, and abilities. We talked about why it's important to appreciate diversity and embrace what makes us unique. We spent quality time discussing LGBTQ issues and the fact that people can identify as what they like because that is acceptable here in Canada. We taught our children that they must respect the views and identifications of others, but that they too have a right to identify as who they are as a Christian male or female and to stay true to their identity and beliefs.

5. Socialization and Peer Interaction

As their school start date approached, we started preparing our children to make friends and engage socially. We talked about sharing, taking turns, and understanding group dynamics. We discussed bullying and discrimination and how to report any such incidents. Our goal was to equip them to recognize red flags, assert their boundaries, and be confident in their voice.

6. Familiarization with the Environment

Since my wife and children arrived in Canada at the end of a school year, we had over two months to explore the new environment before school resumed in September. I wanted to recreate some of the things we did back home to help them adapt. In Lagos we had a regular routine of going for a brisk family walk daily and going swimming every Saturday. So, we started going for walks as a family. We would take off from Paddock Street to Union Street toward Water Street to Broad Street, Crown Street, and back home, looking at monuments and buildings along the way. I showed them where I lived while I was a student during my MBA program, and I pointed out the Loyalist House, the Three Sisters Lamp, the historic Saint John County Court House, Old City Hall of Saint John, the Union Club, King's Square, Queen Square, and the Tidal Steps. These walks provided us an opportunity to bond after we haven't been together for a long time. We studied a map, which enhanced the children's map-reading abilities and gave them the confidence to walk around the city.

These strategies helped us build a new life with old roots—a life where our children could adapt without losing themselves.

In the midst of our adaptation and continuous conversations about change, my youngest daughter Eva wrote the poem below:

Change, it can be good it can be bad
You can be sad and you can be glad

Like the river flowing

And the rocks going

The winds of change begin to hum

A gentle breeze a beating drum

The world around it shifts and sways

In a quiet dance it finds new ways

Key Takeaways

Raising kids in a new environment while helping them navigate culture shock can be a challenging but rewarding experience. As parents, our role is to provide guidance, encouragement, and patience as they adjust to new customs, language, school systems, and social norms. Here are some practical tips I've learned along the way:

1. Create a Safe and Supportive Environment

Start by building a sense of stability and safety at home. Children need to feel seen, heard, and understood as they experience new emotions such as confusion, frustration, or homesickness. Offer reassurance, encouragement, and a calm environment to help them adjust and feel secure through the transition.

2. Acknowledge Their Feelings

Kids may feel overwhelmed by the changes they're experiencing, but they might not always be able to express their emotions clearly. Encourage them to talk about their feelings. Validate how they feel: let them know it's okay to miss home, feel unsure, or even feel upset. Normalizing these feelings helps build their emotional intelligence and resilience.

3. Help Them Build Connections

Social integration is a major part of overcoming culture shock. Encourage your kids to make friends, whether through school, extracurricular activities, or community events. A practical approach is encouraging them to join clubs, sports, or other group activities where they can meet other children and build friendships. A social network will help them feel more comfortable and integrated into their new environment.

4. Introduce the New Culture Gradually

Resist the temptation to overwhelm children with all the cultural differences at once. Introduce the new culture and customs in small, manageable steps. You might start with the holidays, food, sports, or even the weather.

5. Teach Them About Diversity

Multiculturalism is the norm in Canada and many other parts of the world. Teach your children to appreciate the other cultures, perspectives, and traditions they'll encounter. Help them understand that differences are something to be celebrated, not feared.

6. Maintain Connections to Home Culture

While it's important to help kids adapt to a new culture, it's equally important to maintain a connection to their home culture. This can help them feel less disconnected and preserve their sense of identity. Continue celebrating your home traditions, preparing familiar meals, and speaking your native language. These small acts reinforce a sense of continuity and familiarity while they adjust to their new environment.

7. Focus on Positive Aspects of the New Environment

Encourage your children to notice and appreciate the positive aspects of their new surroundings. Whether it's the friendly people, the beauty of the natural landscapes, or fun activities, helping kids focus on the enjoyable parts of their new environment can shift their mindset to a more optimistic outlook on their new life, making it easier for them to embrace the changes around them.

8. Be Patient and Flexible

Lastly, it's essential to be patient with the process. The length of time it takes for kids to fully adjust varies, and there will be setbacks along the way. Flexibility in expectations and a lot of encouragement are key to helping kids thrive in their new environment. Remember that occasional setbacks are part of their growth.

Closing Reflections

Culture shock is inevitable when immigrating to a different place. Adults and kids alike will find many things about their new country or city either odd or amusing. What children need to know is that they can be safe, that they are cared for, and that their family is there for them through all these changes.

"Charles Darwin didn't say that only the strong survive. What he said was that those who survive are the ones who most accurately perceive their environment and successfully adapt to it."
—LEON C. MEGGINSON

CHAPTER SIX:

Career and Job Search

"The best way to predict the future is to invent it."
—ALAN KAY

Like most newcomers, I was both thrilled and petrified upon arriving in my new country. I knew that Canada had a strong economy, a reputation for diversity, and a robust job market, but uneasy questions resounded in my mind: Would I be able to find a suitable job in my field? How would I get my personal and professional groove back?

Back in Lagos, Nigeria, I flourished as a professional in the oil and gas industry. I was a manager in one of the largest oil companies in Nigeria. I was well respected, with bachelor's and master's degrees, multiple certifications, and over a decade of engineering and project management experience. My success was a testament to God's grace, skills, and opportunities that allowed me to grow and thrive professionally.

Upon arriving in Saint John, New Brunswick, for my MBA program, I set a goal to secure a job either before or immediately after completing my MBA.

Everyone in the program had the same anxiety and fear of the unknown regarding finding a job. UNBSJ understood these concerns and organized several professional development sessions to prepare students for future careers in Canada. At these sessions, alumni/ae of the MBA program shared their diverse experiences and perspectives about job hunting. They tried hard, but it seemed to me that none of them was able to lay out a clear path to gainful employment. Several of them said they had received hundreds of rejection letters from different employers across different sectors before finally landing a job.

I was not entirely surprised to hear that. Before leaving Nigeria, I had heard that Saint John was a small city with limited opportunities and few jobs. Once, I went with my brother-in-law Taiwo Adejugbe to the airport to pick up one of his friends. We met a couple more of his friends there, and they jokingly spoke of receiving the "usual" letter of rejection from multiple companies. I cringed when they said that rejections were "the normal thing you hear from employers after an interview."

Finding a suitable job was obviously going to be an uphill task, but in the back of my mind I felt it was not insurmountable. So, I thought to myself: Who can show me the way? What do I need to do, what challenges will I face, and how will I deal with them?

Common Problems for Newcomers Seeking a Job in Canada

I decided to speak to a few persons who had graduated before I arrived or were familiar with the Canadian job market. Their input pointed to the major challenges I would face.

1. Lack of Canadian Work Experience

Top on the list of the hurdles for newcomers is the often-heard phrase "lack of Canadian work experience." No matter how many years of experience and advanced qualifications one brings from abroad, some employers want only people with specific local knowledge, experiences, and credentials. The harsh reality of being an immigrant in a foreign job market is that even the most accomplished professionals can feel invisible. Some recruiters will express admiration for an international background, but that may not be enough to land the kind of opportunity one is hoping for.

The job search often becomes an emotional rollercoaster of interviews that end without an offer and applications that lead nowhere. For those who've worked tirelessly for years building expertise, gaining experience, and earning respect in their home countries, the weight of this obstacle can feel crushing. It's a barrier that often doesn't reflect one's true abilities, talent, or potential but rather the invisible line drawn between "here" and "there", between the place where one's skills are valued and the place where they are judged as foreign. These realities take an emotional toll on internationals as repeated rejections gnaw at their confidence.

In sum, the newcomer to Canada may be facing not just the practical challenge of securing a job but an inner battle over his or her self-worth. *Am I good enough? Did I do something wrong?* It can feel like the success you've worked for and the reputation you've built are somehow not valid anymore.

2. Credential Recognition Issues

Another harsh reality for international professionals is that credentials earned in one country may not be recognized in another. Many newcomers in Canada, despite having advanced degrees from their home countries, find themselves struggling to prove their qualifications in the Canadian job market. Once during my MBA program, I boarded a taxi and got into a conversation with the driver. I was surprised to hear that he had been a highly skilled physician in Asia. Back home, he had spent over a decade saving lives in emergency rooms. He arrived in Canada with his wife and two children, full of hope. But his medical degree was not recognized in Canada. To practice, he would need to pass multiple licensing exams, complete residency training (which had limited spots for international graduates), and pay thousands of dollars in fees. With a family to support, he had no choice but to take up a job as a taxi driver until he was ready to undertake the licensing process.

"I never thought I would be driving strangers around instead of treating patients," he said, his voice heavy with emotion and disappointment. "It feels like everything I worked for has been taken away."

Credential recognition is a major barrier not just for internationally trained doctors but also for nurses, engineers, lawyers, and any profession in which regulatory bodies play a role. Verification processes can take years to complete. Exams, additional coursework, and bridging programs are costly. For some, the process is simply too long and expensive. Hence, they take minimum-wage jobs.

I had practiced as an electrical and instrumentation engineer in Nigeria, so I decided to find out the route to professional engineer (P.Eng.) status in Canada. I was told that it would take three years or more, despite my qualifications and licenses back in Nigeria. I decided to pursue it anyway; the journey is currently in progress.

The impact of credential recognition issues goes beyond careers. It affects mental health, self-worth, and family well-being. Some newcomers often face frustration and even regret over their decision to move. They feel trapped between their past professional identity and their present struggle for survival in jobs that do not utilize their experience.

3. Unfamiliarity with the Job Market

Newcomers who lack awareness of hiring trends in Canada may make mistakes such as neglecting the importance of soft skills. Without proper guidance, newcomers may experience frequent rejections, delayed career progress, and frustration.

4. Unfamiliarity with the Hiring Process

Understanding the Canadian hiring process can be challenging for newcomers.

- **Canadian résumés** are different from those in other countries. In some countries, a CV (curriculum vitae) is customary. A CV is comprehensive and can run six pages or more depending on your years of experience. But in Canada, a résumé is expected to be two pages at most, and professional experience older than ten years should generally be omitted.

- **Cover letters** in Canada customarily strike a certain tone and use verbiage that most newcomers are not familiar with.

- **Interview styles** may be unfamiliar. Depending on the field, one might face panel interviews, behavioral interviews, technical interviews, or stress interviews in addition to the traditional one-on-one interview.

- **Cultural differences around self-promotion** can make some immigrants appear either too modest or too aggressive in an interview, affecting their chances of being hired.

The same goes for how to negotiate salary, how to dress, how to follow up—everything about the process in Canada may be different from what you are used to. These cultural shifts can make the Canadian job market seem impenetrable to newcomers.

5. Discrimination and Unconscious Bias

Despite Canada's multicultural policies, some newcomers often complain of bias in hiring. Some employers may prefer local candidates over those with foreign-sounding names or accents. Implicit bias may lead to assumptions about a candidate's language proficiency, adaptability, work ethic, or ability to fit in. The emphasis on "Canadian experience" might be perfectly legitimate in some fields, while at times it may mask bias and discrimination. These biases, whether intentional or unintentional, force many skilled professionals to take jobs far below their qualifications.

Strategies That Worked for Me

1. Advance Research

I did not wait until the end of my degree program to start preparing for my job search. Far from it! I began researching as soon as I had the thought that I might emigrate.

As I progressed through the MBA program, when talking with instructors, mentors, and friends, I took every appropriate opportunity to inquire about industry trends, challenges in my field, job requirements, and the hiring process.

I used LinkedIn to find out what degrees, certifications, and experience levels are common among professionals in the role I wanted to apply for. Knowing where my deficits were enabled me to work on fixing them.

I went online to check hiring trends and to identify organizations where I wanted to work. Having specific organizations in mind saved me a lot of time and enabled me to focus my efforts on those companies, which enabled me to land my dream job faster.

2. Having Mentors

I had mentors, people I could talk to for advice in making career decisions. Some of them were my MBA instructors. Others were Nigerians whom I met in Canada, and still others were members of my church.

3. Analyzing the Job Market

I analyzed the job market using SWOT analysis—strengths, weaknesses, opportunities, and threats—to understand what could impact my attainment of my goal.

Strengths I identified for myself:

- I was widely traveled with international exposure and experience working in different countries.

- I was experienced in project and operations management. In fact, I had just completed a master's in operations and production management (with distinction) before I moved to Canada.

- I was experienced in leading business transformation, restructuring, quality management, and systems audits.

- My MBA degree enriched my knowledge of business management and leadership beyond managing projects.

- I had project management skills, which were in high demand in Canadian industries including IT, construction, finance, oil and gas, supply chain, and consulting.

- Working various part-time jobs had given me the opportunity to understand the Canadian workplace culture and the Saint John community.

- I was a good communicator and I enjoyed speaking, so stage fright in interviewing and networking situations was not an issue for me.

Weaknesses I identified in myself:

- Perfectionism.

- Fear of failure.

Opportunities I identified:

- I saw clearly that opportunities abounded everywhere. This knowledge is itself an opportunity, because if you assume there are few opportunities, you won't recognize the ones that are there.

- I jotted down the names of about five companies that had openings where my experience would fit, and I followed them closely in the news and online.

- Carbon emission reduction and sustainability are two areas I am passionate about. Having specific areas of interest helped me stand out from the crowd during the application process.

- Canada had several expanding sectors, including tech, infrastructure, and green energy, and project managers were in demand.

- Many companies in Canada had diversity and inclusion initiatives, making it easier for international students to find opportunities.

Threats I identified:

- Competition from many qualified candidates in the local job market, including both recent graduates and experienced professionals.

- Unconscious bias in hiring. I knew that some employers hesitate to hire newcomers due to perceived cultural or communication barriers.

4. Having a Goal

From the beginning of my MBA program, I had a clear goal of getting a job at a reputable company that would get my career back on track. I was clear on the kind of job I wanted (project or operations manager), the companies I wanted to work for, and when I wanted to start work (immediately after graduation).

Because I had done my research, I was less vulnerable to discouragement. I recall a session in my communication class (MBA7510) in which students were paired up to review each other's résumés. My peer in this exercise asserted that I would never get a project manager job in Canada. I said, "No, I can get it." He insisted that he knew what he was talking about and that Canadian employers would not give me a manager role because I was an immigrant or newcomer. I did not let this dissuade me. I was resolute and clear on what I wanted, and I prayed to God and worked toward it by following a purposeful strategy.

As I began applying for jobs, I prioritized applications based on how well they fit my goal. For example, I saw that most of the jobs I was interested in were remote, others were hybrid, and a few were in-person. My top preference was hybrid, with remote second, then in-person last. This knowledge enabled me to prioritize my application efforts.

5. Developing a Strategy

I had outlined the steps to achieve my goals, which were "SMART" (specific, measurable, achievable, relevant, and time-bound).

- Top on my strategy list was to use part-time and coop job opportunities while in school as an opportunity to understand the Canadian workplace culture. For example, during my coop at Saint John Energy, the director took me for lunch, and on our way back to the office I asked him for his thoughts on three organizations which I considered to be top on my list of potential interest. His comments were not only insightful but inspirational. This conversation served as a guiding light throughout the rest of my job hunt.

- I enhanced my LinkedIn profile by using a professional photo, highlighting my skills, and actively engaging with content related to my industry.

- I made a plan to improve my soft skills, because Canadian employers value communication, leadership, and teamwork. This plan included joining the UNBSJ-MBA Graduate Students Association.

6. Implementation and Progress Monitoring

In the midst of competing priorities, I was focused on and committed to implementing my plan. I tracked my progress toward my milestones by checking my list on a weekly basis. Truthfully, the days, weeks, and months rolled by faster than I had expected. I missed a couple of my set milestones, but overall, it was worth the trouble. Progress monitoring ensured I didn't let any areas slide, and it also gave me the confidence that comes from knowing that things were under control.

7. Evaluating Outcomes and Improving

I checked my results roughly once a month, looked for ways I could improve, and incorporated those into my plan.

8. Reinforcing My Vision

During my journey, I kept in mind Philippians 4:13— "I can do all things through Christ who strengthens me." Every time I had the opportunity to speak to anybody about what I wanted to do, I would quickly say that I wanted to work as a project manager at Irving Oil. Each time I passed by the Irving Oil home office building, I would lift up my head, look at it, and say, "I will work here."

"The future depends on what you do today."
—ATTRIBUTED TO MAHATMA GANDHI

Key Takeaways

1. Be Strategic

Do not go through your study journey, or anything else for that matter, without a clearly articulated goal and strategies to achieve your plan. Be continuously forward-thinking. Do not wait for opportunities to come your way or for situations to take you unawares. Plan and prepare, and you will be successful. As the saying goes: opportunity favors the prepared.

2. Avoid Naysayers

Focus on what you believe in and know from your research. Do not allow uninformed people to convince you that you cannot be this or that.

3. Look for Mentors

The importance of having a mentor cannot be overemphasized. Having multiple mentors is like having a personal board of directors. Each one has areas of expertise that they are willing to share.

An ideal mentor is someone with experience you lack who is happy to answer questions and offer guidance. To find a mentor, talk with people you meet. Ask a question and listen earnestly to the reply. People who respond enthusiastically to a question and go on to offer more advice may eventually become great mentors for you. Cultivate these relationships by showing appreciation, taking sincere interest in things the other person enjoy, and offering your own knowledge in return.

4. Get Needed Credentials

Use LinkedIn and talk with mentors and your network to learn what credentials are expected for the kind of job you want. Depending on your field, consider relevant certifications such as PMP, PRINCE2, Agile, CFA, CPA, CPHR, PROSCI, DevOps or ITIL. In some fields, certifications may be a vital necessity. Even if that is not the case in your field, certifications will help you stand out.

5. Manage Your Professional Profiles

- Enhance your LinkedIn profile by using a professional photo and highlighting your skills. Update it regularly as you obtain needed credentials. Actively engage with industry-related content and your organizations of interest.

- Ensure that your résumé, your LinkedIn profile, and your other social media platforms are all consistent.

- Connect thoughtfully on career and social platforms, not just widely. Engage consistently, create value-driven content, stay in touch with people you interact with, and leverage events and webinars.

- Besides LinkedIn, other platforms for networking and job searching include Glassdoor, Job Bank Canada (the government jobs portal), and company websites (apply directly through career pages). There are also specialized networking hubs for specific industries. Evaluate them carefully and participate if the interactions you see there appear worthwhile.

6. Improve Your Soft Skills

Canadian employers value communication, leadership, and teamwork, sometimes even more than your technical skills. You can improve your soft skills in many ways. Formal methods could include joining Toastmasters club, attending networking events with a more experienced colleague and watching how they conduct themselves, volunteering in the community, or working a part-time job. Informal methods could include simply setting a goal to talk to one new person each day or asking a mentor to recommend books about relevant soft skills.

7. Start Applying Early

If you are a student, do not wait to graduate from school before actively applying for jobs. I was going to graduate in October, but I started applying for jobs in June and had three job offers by August. Starting early means that you have enough time to correct mistakes and practice without too much pressure or anxiety. Each interview gives you experience that you can apply to the next interview.

8. Optimize Your Résumé Strategy

- Avoid submitting generic applications. Tailor each résumé to the job description—but be completely honest.

- Remember that your résumé should be limited to your last ten years of work experience and should not be more than two pages in length. If needed, you can shorten your résumé by removing the experience and education that are less relevant to the job in question. However, be careful not to create the impression that you've had a long gap in your employment history if that is not the case.

- Ensure that your résumé contains achievements and not just a list of jobs you have held. Hiring managers want to see what you have achieved in your career experience relevant to the role you have applied for.

- Use available resources such as Saint John Newcomer Centre and writing centre or input from mentors to vet your résumé before submission. I often hear people say, "I have submitted hundreds of résumés, yet I rarely get called to interview." If you find yourself in this situation, it is possible that your résumé did not match the role, or the hiring manager didn't see what they were looking for in your résumé. A trusted vetter may be able to help you fix such issues.

9. Prepare for Interviews

- Prepare for behavioral questions during interviews. Use the STAR method (Situation, Task, Action, Result) to answer questions about competency or experience. Competency-based questions are often used by employers to test whether your professed work history is true and authentic.

- Practice! Practice! Practice! Have a helper ask you interview questions, and make an effort to be concise and clear in your responses. Practice speaking with confidence.

- Use YouTube to find examples of how to describe your past experience in a clear and effective way. This can help you find the right terminology and even sentence structure to use. Describing your experience well is important because many employers focus more on their talent gaps and their bottom line than on having a rapport with the applicant. It is not enough to make an emotional connection; you must communicate that you are fit for the role.

10. Follow Up After Every Interview

Always demonstrate your professionalism by sending a thank-you email after each interview. Affirm your interest in the position, further buttress your relevant experience, and restate the value you will deliver to the company if hired. Demonstrate enthusiasm about the organization, the role, and your potential team. Tell them that you can't wait to join the team and do your part in helping the organization achieve its goals.

11. Be Flexible

Be open to alternative pathways to achieving your career goals. For example:

- If you have your eye on a manager role, don't let that preclude you from applying for roles lower than management level, especially if you have never had a management role before. Sometimes beginning from where you are is very valuable in getting your foot in the door.

Most organizations "promote from within," meaning they move their most capable employees into roles of greater responsibility rather advertising every job opening.

- Consider freelance or contract jobs.

- If you are still struggling to find a job at the level you desire in your field, consider a stepping-stone job that can lead you to the role you want.

- Consider a career switch that aligns with your values and passions.

- Consider relocating. Some provinces and cities have a higher demand for skilled workers or fewer job seekers than others. If you are in a large city with a large applicant pool, consider a smaller city where the competition for positions may be less fierce.

Alternate pathways to employment will help you gain Canadian experience, and that's always a plus.

12. Set Goals, Monitor Your Progress, and Check Your Results

Set goals and make plans to achieve them, as I've discussed throughout this book. Once you've begun to implement your plan, do not forget to check whether what you are doing is working. Step back regularly to review your progress. Look for things you can do differently to address challenges.

13. Visualize

Review chapter two about vision casting. Have a vision and reinforce it daily.

14. Persist and Maintain a Positive Mindset

Persistence and resilience are key. Learn from rejections and improve continuously. Engage resilience and flexibility to navigate challenges. Don't be too hard on yourself.

15. Improve Language Skills and Work to Adapt to the Culture

Strong English (or French) skills and an understanding of Canadian workplace culture can set you apart. If you are new to Canada, try these strategies:

- Tune in to radio and television programs featuring news and other general discussions. From these, you can learn communication skills and nuances such as vocal variety and word registers. These skills will help you gain confidence in speaking.

- Follow communication experts on social media.

- Consider joining Toastmasters club. It has been very useful in my public speaking and communications journey; it might help you as well.

"A career is like a garden in that it, too, requires plenty of plotting and planning, lots of preliminary spadework, the right seeds sown in the right soil, and a long period of careful cultivation."
—Phyllis I. Rosenteur

Closing Reflections

To every immigrant or newcomer, I'd say be clear on what kind of work you want and where. When you have a clear, specific, and well researched goal, you can focus your efforts on it. This will help you maximize your opportunities, reduce the amount of pressure you feel, and ultimately save you time. And don't let naysayers distract and discourage you from your goal.

Securing a job in Canada as an international requires a deliberate and strategic approach. By combining networking, continuous learning, and persistence, internationals can successfully transition to employment in Canada. What works is to stay proactive, take advantage of opportunities that support your vision, and ask for help from mentors, career advisors, and professional connections. Internationals should focus on gaining local experience, obtaining relevant certifications, and leveraging government programs. Adapting to market trends, improving communication skills, and staying persistent can significantly improve job prospects in Canada.

"Success is the sum of small efforts, repeated day in and day out."
—Florence Taylor

CHAPTER SEVEN

Building Your Network

"Your network is your net worth."
—Porter Gale

In Canada, as in many other places, the job market is not solely based on qualifications and experience. Who you know is often just as important as what you know. Some job openings are not publicly advertised; instead, they are filled through referrals and internal recommendations. Some employers prefer to hire through referrals because the referrer provides some assurance that the candidate will be a good fit for the company culture. This takes some of the risk out of hiring.

All these put the newcomer at an immediate disadvantage: even if they are highly qualified, they may never get a chance to apply for a job that isn't advertised. Even when a job is advertised, the newcomer's application may get lost in the digital void, sometimes because the applicant lacks the requirements of a Canadian standard resume or a suitable referrer.

In light of the above, networking plays a crucial role in hiring in Canada. Research shows that business and professional networks often lead to more job and business opportunities, broader and deeper knowledge, improved capacity to innovate, faster advancement, and greater status and authority. Building and nurturing professional relationships also improves the quality of work through peer review.

Unfortunately, networking outside one's immediate academic or cultural community can be a real challenge for immigrants or newcomers. Access to professional mentorship programs and adequate alumni networks may be limited. Some immigrants may not know how to use LinkedIn effectively or approach networking events with confidence.

When thought leaders emphasize the importance of networking, the "how" is often lacking. Have you ever attended a networking event where you felt completely lost and wondered what you were doing there? How about beating the rain and snow only to feel that the networking event was a total waste of your time? Have you ever been in a crowded hall but had no idea who was in the room or what you should be doing or saying? Such was my experience at many networking events. The "how" of networking is seldom taught, and this is a big need among newcomers navigating the job market.

I recall a networking event during my MBA program at the University of New Brunswick. The room was packed with students, newcomers, and representatives of various organizations. Yet many of the newcomers in the hall felt out of place. They didn't know anyone in the room other than the organizers, and starting a conversation with a stranger seemed like a nearly impossible task. I noticed that as soon as a senior faculty member of the university walked in, most students gravitated toward her, hoping to ease their tension. She waved them off kindly but firmly, saying, "You already know me. Go talk to the many other people in the hall and make new connections." To my dismay, the pack of students withdrew and all stood aloof, not knowing what to do. The students ended up chatting with themselves, and the guests talked only with other guests. It seemed like a waste of time for everyone involved.

As I watched the room, I felt sad and dejected. I was worried about why some newcomers with numerous years of experience found this singular important activity so difficult to do. That was when it struck me that many books and speakers describe the benefits of networking but say little about how to do it. Someone needs to teach the "how." For newcomers navigating a different culture, the "how" is very important.

Networking Phobia

Many times, I have heard people say, "I hate networking!" Even executives and other professionals say it. Why do people find it so difficult? What could be the cause of such extreme discomfort?

Different people have different reasons. You have probably heard some or all of the following at one time or another:

- "Networking is for extroverts, people who have a flair for social situations and chatting. I'm an introvert."

- "I feel like a beggar when I try to network."

- "Networking is so phony and exploitative."

Newcomers are no different; many of them feel the same way. But on top of those very common objections, newcomers face extra challenges when networking:

- **Cultural Differences.** What networking looks like varies from culture to culture. In some cultures, networking is more formal or professional, while in others, it's more personal. Newcomers often find it difficult to navigate this unfamiliar space, sometimes because of a fear of being judged for their background or their unfamiliarity with local norms. For example, having come from a communal culture, I found it difficult at first to network in an individualistic culture where personal space is valued and physical contact is minimal. Cultural differences can be a major obstacle to successful networking.

- **Language Barriers.** Networking requires communication, and communication in a language one is not fluent in can be intimidating and frustrating. At one of the many networking events I attended, I observed that some newcomers in the hall who were not fluent in English (understandably, because it was not the primary language in their home country) felt critically self-conscious about their ability to express themselves clearly. The challenge of interpreting thoughts and cues in their native language before translating them to the English language without losing the information they were trying to convey was obvious. When the locals struggled to keep up with their communication due to incorrect tenses or sentence structure, the newcomers felt even more uncomfortable.

- **Accents.** Newcomers with an accent often feel self-conscious during networking events. They may fear being judged, misunderstood, or perceived as less capable because they lack the local accent. Constantly being asked, "Where are you from?" can shift the focus of conversation away from the newcomer's skills and experience. All these factors can result in self-doubt, anxiety, and reluctance to approach others.

- **Prejudice and Bias:** Prejudice and bias often discourage newcomers from networking. For example, newcomers who may have experienced discrimination or exclusion in social or professional settings might avoid networking in order to prevent negative experiences or feelings of not fitting in. This leads to feelings of isolation, making it even harder to initiate connections or build trust. Fear of not being accepted often prevents newcomers from fully engaging in social situations.

The above challenges, and more, often diminish the newcomer's willingness to network. It's understandable: no one likes to feel awkward, incapable, excluded, overlooked, unwelcome, or underestimated based on their nationality, accent, or cultural background. That said, I believe the narrative can be changed.

Key Takeaways

Many of us, especially newcomers, need help to make networking easier, more authentic, and more effective. Within my profession and my areas of interest, I have built and continue to build strong relationships that have been instrumental to my career success and visibility. Here are strategies that helped me, and could help you, build strong, and lasting connections:

1. Know Your Purpose

You don't need to attend every event, just the ones that align with your goals and values. Ask yourself:

- What is the purpose of the event?

- Does the event align with my career or business goals?

- Will I meet people connected to my area of interest?

- Will the event be attended by the organizations and individuals who will have a direct impact on my career?

Attend only the events that align with your goals. This will make it easier to decline invitations. For example, if you are not a farmer and agribusiness is not your goal, you do not need to be at a networking event for farmers. On the other hand, whenever you find an event that is aligned with your career plans, make every effort to clear your calendar and attend.

2. Prepare Ahead of Time

- **Optimize your LinkedIn profile.** LinkedIn is the primary website where people will go to look you up after a networking event, so optimize your LinkedIn profile before the event. Also, make sure you are posting thoughtfully on LinkedIn, not just widely, but engage and reply consistently. (Side note: LinkedIn is one way to find networking opportunities, including both in-person events and webinars.)

- **Build a strong online presence** that includes not just LinkedIn but other platforms, such as X (formerly Twitter), Bluesky, Facebook, and Instagram. Not only does this make it easier for others to find you, it also helps people to learn more about your career path and connect with you more often. Update your online identity, or brand, and ensure that it is consistent across all your social media platforms.

- **Research the people and companies you want to meet.** Once you've identified a networking event that is right for you, research the speakers and other attendees to identify the ones you most want to meet. What are their roles? What might you have in common? Advance research will enable you to ask more insightful questions and discover more about the individual, the workplace, and the company.

- **Prepare a brief, clear self-introduction** that highlights your strengths and interests. This is often called an icebreaker or an elevator pitch. Make it memorable and clear. Practice saying it until it flows naturally. Let it include who you are, what you do, and what you're looking to achieve. Always be ready to give your pitch, but make sure it flows like conversation and not like a recitation of a memorized "spiel."

- **Be ready to exchange business cards or electronic contact details** with other attendees.

- **Look for ways to give as well as take.** Listen and contribute to discussions rather than concentrating only on what you can get from the event. Networking is a rare opportunity for people to get to know you. Listen actively and show genuine interest in others. Being respectful, enthusiastic, and authentic helps you stand out and leaves a lasting, positive impression on potential employers, mentors, and collaborators.

3. Present Yourself Well

How you present yourself during a networking event is crucial, as first impressions often shape professional opportunities. A confident, polished demeanor communicates credibility and professionalism.

- Dress appropriately for the event, and maintain good posture.

- When introducing yourself, stand upright, use a firm handshake, and make eye contact. If you're wearing a nametag, point to it.

- Have the right mindset about networking. A networking event is an opportunity to connect with people and build long-lasting relationships. Go in to connect, to listen, and to start relationships—not to ask for a job. It's possible you could be offered a job on the spot, but it is highly unlikely, so that should not be your main focus. People generally want to get to know you as a way of building a relationship. Entering a networking event with a mindset of getting a job would make you appear desperate and inauthentic.

- Preparation and confidence are key. Show gratitude for the event in your conversations. Speak about how valuable the event is to you. Speak well of the organizers and the good job they have done rather than complaining or pointing out the flaws in the event. Avoid negative energy.

4. Think Broadly About What You Can Give

Newcomers are often tempted to think they have nothing to offer during a networking event. Focusing on what you don't have will make you feel powerless, and this may consequently weaken your resolve to connect with others. Even when you do not share the same historical background with someone, you can probably find something valuable to offer by thinking beyond the obvious. Of course, this isn't always easy. Remember that, as newcomers, we possess a wealth of experience both professionally and otherwise. We have wonderful stories to tell that would inspire our new friends. We often come with resilience, grit, fresh perspectives, positive energy, and warmth. These are valuable gifts that we can give to new relationships as we develop them.

5. Break the Ice

For many people, few things are scarier than approaching someone they don't know at an event. After the networking event I described at the beginning of this chapter, the feedback from most of my friends was that they didn't know what to say to a stranger. This was a fair and valid point because they did not know what their common interests with others might be.

My recommendation is to start by introducing yourself. My line was, "Hi, my name is Isaac. I am originally from Nigeria. I am an MBA student at the University of New Brunswick Saint John. I have experience in project and operations management, and I am looking forward to building a career in project management after I graduate."

Another icebreaker I used was, "Hi, my name is Isaac. I hope you are having a good time at this event. I am an MBA student, and I am attending this event to connect and build relationships within the community because I really like Saint John and would like to settle here after my program. What about you?"

An icebreaker opens up the conversation—that is, assuming you have done a bit of research into the event, the organizers, and the potential attendees. Preparation is key.

6. What If I Am an Introvert?

Networking isn't only for extroverts. As long as you can speak, you can develop confidence in speaking to new people. If nothing else, just muster the courage to say hello. Remember that the ability to connect and interact is a vital skill in working almost everywhere, including Canada. So, use networking events as an opportunity to practice what you will eventually do in your place of work. Try these tips:

- Attend with a friend who is comfortable with networking and observe how they interact. This gives you the opportunity to learn the ropes without being the center of attention.

- Practice a few lines you're comfortable saying. For example, a simple 'Hello' with your hand extended for a handshake demonstrates confidence and friendship. Do that, then allow the conversation flow from there.

- Volunteer for causes or organizations where you can connect naturally. Volunteering in your area of interest gives you the visibility and opportunity to showcase your experiences and talents and build a network.

- Start by attending virtual networking events. These are sometimes easier to manage and not as overwhelming as the in-person ones.

Remember that networking isn't about being the loudest person in the room but about being intentional and authentic.

7. Stay in Touch

The networking process does not end when the career event or job fair is over. Be sure to give and receive contact information, then follow up with your new contacts to continue the relationship and preserve the connections. If you are inviting someone to connect on LinkedIn, for example, personalize the note field in the invitation to remind the person where you met. Avoid the temptation to ask for a job as soon as you connect. It makes you appear to be a "user," someone who shamelessly takes and never gives. Allow the relationship to grow organically.

Closing Reflections

Many of us are ambivalent about networking. We know that it's critical to our personal and professional development, yet we find it challenging and often distasteful. I hope that the tips presented in this chapter will help you overcome your aversion. By shifting your mindset, identifying and exploring shared interests, expanding your view of what you have to offer, and motivating yourself with a purpose, you'll become more excited about networking and more effective at building valuable relationships of mutual benefit.

For those who organize events that include newcomers, you can support this group by creating structure. For example, have an agenda, deliver some opening remarks, and introduce participants or organizations. Providing context ahead of time is very helpful. A list of expected attendees and organizations will enable everyone to prepare adequately. With the right support, preparation, and practice, newcomers can gradually build confidence with networking and thrive in professional settings.

To the thought leaders, mentors, and academic instructors, don't focus only on the "what" and "why" of networking. Teach the "how" as well, so newcomers are better prepared to network successfully.

"The most important thing in networking is building relationships, not just swapping business cards."
—Karen S. O'Connor

CHAPTER EIGHT:
Navigating Workplace Dynamics

"Adaptability is the simple secret of survival."
—Jessica Hagedorn

In Canada and anywhere else, successfully navigating the workplace and building strong connections with colleagues require a mix of professionalism, cultural awareness, and interpersonal skills.

Following are some of my experiences with workplace dynamics in Canada.

Early in my MBA program, I was already researching organizations where I thought I might want to work. I identified a few companies that aligned with my values and career trajectory, and I pinned them on my vision board. One of these was Irving Oil Limited. With its hundred-year history and its status as the largest refinery in Canada, Irving had stood out to me since my very first operations management class in the MBA program.

I knew that navigating the Canadian job market as a newcomer, especially in a specialized industry like energy, would require patience, strategy, and a lot of resilience. Each time I passed by the Irving Oil home office in Saint John, New Brunswick, I would pray and confess faith.

I began my employment search in earnest as my MBA program was winding down, amidst hope and trust in God for the next phase of my journey.

After several months of adapting my résumé to meet Canadian standards, attending job fairs, and connecting with professionals on LinkedIn, I made a first attempt at Irving Oil which did not work out as expected. Although I was disappointed, I gained a lot of insights about some of my expectations that had previously been vague.

Later on, I came across a project management opening at Irving. The role aligned well with my previous experience overseas, and I made sure to tailor my application to highlight relevant skills, achievements, and certifications (like PMP). I also included a cover letter that explained my relocation to Canada and my enthusiasm to contribute my international experience to the team.

To my delight, I received a call back within two weeks. The first stage of interviewing was conducted by the HR business partner, followed by the hiring manager. They asked situational and behavioral questions about conflict resolution, stakeholder management, and my ability to deliver projects within schedule and budget.

What stood out to me about Irving was the openness to diversity and inclusion at every stage of the recruitment process. They appreciated my global experience and were curious about how my perspective could enrich the team.

And so, on November 8, 2023, I walked through the doors of a building I had long admired from afar to begin my job at Irving. Receiving my employee ID card on that fateful Wednesday was the culmination of years of dreaming, praying, preparing, and networking.

My manager had sent me a detailed plan for my first day. He received me in the front lobby and escorted me to my new office.

Adjusting to the Job

After a few days of excitement, it was time to settle into my role in project management, working in the energy transition space. As part of my onboarding, I was paired with a buddy—another project manager who helped me get familiar with internal tools, teams, and processes. Days turned to weeks and weeks into months. No two days were ever the same.

While fascinating, energy transition projects are extremely dynamic. Unlike conventional oil and gas projects, which tend to be more predictable with well-established processes and robust frameworks, energy transition projects are often fluid. The technology evolves rapidly, regulatory frameworks shift frequently, and stakeholders (both external and internal) bring diverse, sometimes conflicting expectations. Keeping these projects moving requires constant communication to align expectations, manage risks proactively, and maintain a transparent feedback loop.

Although every energy transition project presents unique difficulties, they are all united by the need to manage uncertainty in the interest of energy efficiency and a more sustainable future.

Team dynamics also play a crucial role in my field, highlighting the importance of "soft skills." As a project manager, I've discovered that managing change involves not just technology, but people. I've worked with engineers, financial analysts, supply management experts, compliance managers, etc., each with a different lens through which they view success. As the project manager, my job is to create cohesion, ensure we're all speaking the same language, and keep everyone focused on the bigger picture.

I must say that I have been blessed to work in an amazing organization with some of the best colleagues and managers who have supported me in diverse ways to succeed.

Essential Skills for Workplace Success

To thrive in a professional setting, especially as a newcomer, it's not enough to have technical expertise alone. Here are a few soft skills I believe are critical to workplace success in most organizations:

1. Attitude and Body Language

Your attitude and nonverbal communication can play a major role in how you're perceived. Do you show up with a positive attitude and enthusiasm for your work? This goes a long way toward building credibility and nurturing professional relationships.

Body language is also very key. Making eye contact, smiling, and maintaining good posture during conversations and meetings communicates confidence and engagement. Nodding while someone speaks, leaning slightly forward, or using open hand gestures can signal attentiveness and interest. On the flip side, closed-off or passive body language, like avoiding eye contact, folding arms, or looking distracted, might be interpreted as disinterest or unwillingness to collaborate, even when it's unintended.

2. Communication

Clear, respectful communication is essential for professionals to succeed in any workplace and maintain their employment long term. It fosters trust, minimizes misunderstandings, and strengthens workplace relationships.

Many proficient newcomer professionals find it difficult to ask questions, give feedback, or express ideas in a way that conforms to the workplace norms. But asking questions, requesting clarification, and being open to feedback are nonetheless important because they show initiative, a willingness to learn, and a desire to grow.

Speaking up during meetings, contributing ideas in a professional manner, and offering thoughtful input demonstrate confidence and teamwork. Cultural differences in expression can sometimes lead to misunderstandings, so it's helpful to observe how others interact and mirror positive behaviors. Being mindful of your tone and observing how others interact can help you fit into team dynamics more smoothly.

3. Punctuality

Punctuality is a highly regarded soft skill that is crucial for the retention and success of newcomer professionals in any workplace, including the Canadian workplace. Being punctual for work, meetings, and deadlines demonstrates professionalism, dependability, and respect. It shows that you take your obligations seriously and are someone others can count on. Many employers view punctuality as a sign of dedication and strong organizational skills. On the other hand, frequent lateness can undermine trust and raise questions about your work ethic. You might be perceived as inconsiderate and disrespectful of other people's time if you always show up late. Oftentimes Canadians in part-time as well as full-time positions like to plan and execute like clockwork. Tardiness disrupts that flow and leads to multiple ripple effects. There is no doubt that being reliably on time enhances your reputation and helps prevent negative perceptions regarding time management.

4. Collaboration

Exhibiting a cooperative attitude and a willingness to collaborate with others can significantly improve job stability and mutual respect in the Canadian workplace. Generally, the work culture promotes mutual support for the team's success. Strong teamwork abilities facilitate integration, foster healthy connections, and enable each team member to make significant contributions to shared goals. If you're new to the environment, you can demonstrate your collaborative mindset by actively participating in team activities, listening to others, and offering assistance. As trust grows, your colleagues will be more likely to include and support you in projects. Remember that no two persons are alike. Some colleagues may be more reserved and others more outgoing. Adapt your approach accordingly. Along with opening doors to career advancement and mentoring, collaboration can also help you avoid isolation, which is a common struggle with newcomers.

It's important to note that collaboration does not mean leaving your own task undone to help others. I once heard of a supervisor at a financial institution who got terminated after focusing too heavily on helping an understaffed team. While her heart was in the right place, she paid too much attention to others' responsibilities to the detriment of her own. This resulted in her falling behind on her own key performance indicators. Balance is essential.

5. Visibility

Sustaining your career requires more than simply showing up. It requires being visible. Visibility builds trust and opens doors to mentoring, leadership opportunities, and career progression.

Ways to be visible include contributing during meetings, exchanging ideas, and demonstrating leadership in modest ways. Take initiative, track and showcase your wins, seek new challenges, volunteer, and be responsible. Particularly in collaborative settings, working quietly in isolation can cause others to overlook your contributions or misunderstand your role. If you are a supervisor or manager, acknowledging the contributions of your team members can go a long way toward boosting morale and retention. Immigrant professionals become more visible and gain trust when they speak up, participate in cross-functional projects, volunteer for internal committees, and openly communicate their successes.

6. Personal and Professional Development

One of the most common mistakes professionals make after landing a job is settling in without pursuing further personal and professional growth. Continual personal and professional development is key to long-term success and job retention in any progressive workplace. If you constantly improve your skills, whether through formal training, certifications, or informal peer learning, you will be able to display flexibility and a dedication to development. Employers highly value individuals who take the initiative to advance their knowledge and keep up with industry changes. It tells them that you're proactive and committed to your position, which increases the likelihood of being noticed for advancement. Developing skills like emotional intelligence, communication, and leadership can help you navigate cultural differences more effectively. Sharing lessons from professional development opportunities with your colleagues and your manager further demonstrates leadership and initiative. It also boosts your profile within the organization and shows you're invested in your role.

7. Workplace Networking and Relationship Building

For you to succeed in your workplace and keep your job, networking and relationship-building are crucial. Developing close relationships with co-workers, managers, and peers in your field promotes cooperation, trust, and support for one another. Better communication, more seamless teamwork, and greater visibility inside an organization are frequently the results of positive partnerships. Additionally, networking gives you access to opportunities, guidance, and important information that may not be public knowledge. When challenges arise in the workplace, having allies can make a significant difference in how issues are handled or resolved. Without allies, you are more likely to be "thrown under the bus" when a problem arises. Make efforts to identify common interests, especially with your manager. Find out what they like and what they do besides work. Research and learn about their interests so that your conversation is not limited to work alone. You will more likely be perceived as involved, trustworthy, and culturally integrated if you take the effort to establish sincere relationships. In addition to providing a safety net during uncertain employment periods, strong professional networks facilitate more seamless and purposeful career growth.

Key Takeaways

1. Don't Be Excessively Formal or Hierarchical

Some work cultures might still operate in a hierarchical system, but most Canadian workplaces tend to be informal and flat rather than hierarchical. It could come across as awkward or distant to address your manager as "Sir" or "Ma'am." First names are almost always fine, even with senior colleagues, unless you are advised otherwise. Study your work environment and adapt to the culture there.

2. Speak Up and Share Ideas

It could be detrimental to remain silent at meetings, to refrain from asking questions, or to constantly profess total agreement with others' opinions. One of my mentors told me, "If you were invited to the meeting, you are expected to have an opinion." In this part of the world, employers often value participation, initiative, and collaboration. Silence could be mistaken for disinterest or lack of confidence. Rather than being quiet, ask questions or offer supporting information. Don't make yourself the center of attention by talking too much, but do all you can to avoid being completely silent during a meeting.

3. Emphasize Teamwork, Not Qualifications

When interacting with colleagues, don't constantly mention your degrees, past titles, or experience. This may come off as boastful or out of touch in a work culture that values humility and collaboration. Focus instead on how your skills contribute to team success.

4. Learn to Converse and Make Small Talk

Skipping lunch with coworkers, not engaging in chit-chat, or avoiding after-work events might seem harmless, but these choices can lead to isolation and lack of trust. In many workplaces, trust is built through casual conversations in the lobby, after meetings, or even in the elevator. Being distant during seemingly inconsequential moments can lead to being excluded at important ones. Join in small talk. A few minutes of friendly chat can strengthen your professional relationships.

5. Learn to Be Direct Yet Polite

Striking the right tone can be tricky. Being too blunt may come off as rude, while being too vague may seem evasive or unassertive. Canadians generally appreciate polite but direct communication. Use softeners such as "I wonder if . . ." or "What do you think about . . ." to strike a respectful tone while sharing ideas.

6. Ask for Help or Clarification When Needed

The temptation to try to figure everything out on your own to avoid looking weak is common to new hires. This could cause mistakes or make you appear disengaged. In Canadian work culture, asking for help is seen as a responsible act. It shows you care about doing things the right way and that you're engaged in your role. Don't be afraid to ask questions.

7. Accept Feedback Gracefully

Taking constructive criticism personally or being too passive in resolving conflicts makes you come across as lacking emotional intelligence. Feedback is common and expected. Avoid viewing it as an attack. Instead, see it as a professional tool for improvement. If it's not clear to you what you are being asked to do differently, say: "Can you help me understand how I can improve?"

8. Maintain Work–Life Balance

Working excessively long hours or sending emails outside of work hours may not be seen as signs of dedication. They could be viewed as symptoms of poor time management or even lack of consideration for your colleagues. To avoid burnout and reduced productivity, you must set healthy boundaries, take breaks, and make use of vacation or personal days to recharge and maintain long-term effectiveness. If you work late, schedule your emails to send at normal business hours. Respect boundaries regarding after-work communication. If you come from a background where it is normal to contact colleagues about work after work hours, you might want to find out if it is acceptable in your new workplace. While Canadians work hard, they also value personal time and mental wellness.

Closing Reflection

Navigating the Canadian workplace as a newcomer is a journey of learning, adaptation, and resilience. Whether it's mastering small talk, embracing workplace politeness, overcoming language barriers, standing up for fairness, or participating in social events, success begins with understanding the landscape and showing up with purpose.

For every immigrant who has ever felt uncertain, out of place, or overwhelmed in a new workplace, remember—you are not alone. With patience, deliberate effort, and an open mind, you can thrive in Canada's work environment or any other work environment.

"The real office language isn't English or French—i
t's reading between the lines."
—Anonymous

CHAPTER NINE

Navigating the Entrepreneurship Landscape

"Entrepreneurship is not about taking risks—it's about managing them with courage and clarity."
—HOWARD STEVENSON, HARVARD BUSINESS SCHOOL

Many newcomers land in Canada and bring with them decades of experience of running successful businesses in their home countries. Whether they run a start-up or have bought an existing business, immigrants often come with ambitions, confidence, and a dream to translate their previous unique experiences into flourishing business empires.

While the entrepreneurial spirit among immigrants is high, the reality of doing business in Canada requires navigating a complex landscape shaped by cultural, financial, regulatory, and social barriers. Will business practices that worked in their home countries translate directly into the Canadian context? How different are Canadian consumer preferences, business etiquette, legal structures, and marketing norms from those they have known before? This chapter examines the experiences of entrepreneurs, including opportunities they have explored, how they navigated their new business landscape, challenges they faced, and what they learned.

Let's hear from the lived experiences of some entrepreneurs.

Oluwatosin Ezekiel, CEO of DOTS Event Planning

Moving to Saint John, New Brunswick, was one of the hardest transitions of my life. I arrived from Nigeria with my two-year-old daughter, full of uncertainty, hope, and fear. I didn't know anyone, and for a while, I truly couldn't see how I would survive. Everything was new. New country, new weather, new systems. But deep down, I knew I had to keep going.

I came to Saint John to pursue my MBA. Balancing my studies and my new life as a young mom was not easy. I applied for daycare, but there was no space available. I was placed on a long wait list. I remember struggling to focus in class while my toddler was by my side. It was overwhelming!

Thankfully, a few other student parents and I came together and decided to support each other. Some had daytime classes, while others attended at night, so we created a childcare rotation system that made it easier for all of us to attend our lectures. That simple arrangement became a lifeline and a beautiful reminder that even when you have no family around, it is possible to build a supportive community.

Another place that gave me comfort was Trinity Anglican Church. As an Anglican by birth, I naturally found my way there. Reverend Steven welcomed me warmly, and I met wonderful people, including the Olands, Jim Brittain, and Jennifer

Waldschutz. They helped me settle in and proved that kindness can cross cultures and continents.

As I continued my studies, the thought of returning to business kept tugging at my heart. I had run an event planning company in Nigeria, and I loved creating joyful experiences. Still, I wondered: Would it work here? Would anyone book me in this new place?

But passion has a way of pushing through fear. I conducted surveys, did my research, and finally decided to take a leap of faith. I sold my business in Nigeria to raise capital and used that to launch DOTS Event Planning here in Saint John. I started with small indoor parties and relied heavily on word of mouth and referrals at first. Slowly but surely, the bookings began to come in.

The game changer was introducing a 360-degree photobooth—a unique service that stood out in the local market and became a hit at events. It helped give my business an identity, and it drew attention to the full range of services we offered.

There were tough times and days I wanted to give up, but my passion and faith kept me going. I believed in what I was building.

Today, DOTS Event Planning is known for event décor, photo booths, and creative party solutions. From a quiet beginning to a growing brand, my journey is proof that with resilience, faith, and the right people around you, success is possible.

To every immigrant or young mom with a dream: it's okay to start small. You don't need to have it all figured out. Just start and keep going.

Christine Eruokwu
Founder, Kaima Designs
Director, United Colour of Fashion (UCOF)

I launched Kaima Designs in 2017 as an African-inspired fashion brand, rooted in a desire to celebrate and share my cultural heritage with my local community. More than a creative outlet, Kaima Designs became a platform for purpose, supporting the education of vulnerable girls in West Africa through proceeds from our collections.

In 2021, driven by a shared vision, I co-founded the United Colours of Fashion (UCOF) with my friend Rufina Ajalie. UCOF was created to empower immigrants and increase the visibility of minority groups in New Brunswick, many of whom face systemic barriers to accessing vocational training, education, employment, and entrepreneurship. Through mentorship, training, and inclusive programming, UCOF provides a vital space for underserved communities to thrive and lead.

Like many Black entrepreneurs in New Brunswick, I have faced significant challenges in building and sustaining my business. Access to capital remains one of the biggest obstacles—not just for startup costs, but for long-term growth and stability. While organizations such as the Black Business and Professional Network, the Foundation for Black Communities, the Black Business Initiative, and Tribe Network provide meaningful support, much of the assistance focuses on capacity-building— such as access to legal, marketing, accounting, and website development services. However, the direct funding or working capital business owners need to scale operations or expand into new markets is often lacking.

In the fashion industry specifically, shipping costs present another hurdle. Shipping costs from the maritime provinces to the rest of Canada and beyond, particularly for heavier or bulkier products, are prohibitively high, making it difficult to reach customers outside the region or even within Canada without absorbing losses. This limits our ability to grow our customer base and compete nationally or globally.

Due to these persistent barriers, many Black entrepreneurs are forced to maintain full-time jobs while operating their businesses as side hustles. This dual responsibility means we often work long hours, juggling multiple roles without adequate support. In many cases, we depend heavily on volunteers to fill gaps in expertise—whether it's in marketing, logistics, or administration.

Fortunately, resources like ConnexionWorks have been instrumental in helping bridge some of these knowledge and support gaps. Through training workshops and networking opportunities, they create spaces where entrepreneurs can learn, grow, and connect with potential partners or clients.

Still, the path remains steep. Building a business as a Black entrepreneur in New Brunswick often requires more than determination. It demands resilience, resourcefulness, and a strong support system. My journey with Kaima Designs and UCOF continues to be one of purpose and perseverance, driven by the belief that with the right support, we can overcome these barriers and build businesses that empower others and inspire change.

For immigrants like me, navigating the entrepreneurship landscape, especially in smaller communities like Saint John, can be incredibly rewarding but also filled with unique challenges. Here are practical tips and advice to help make the path more manageable and successful:

1. Start with What You Know and Love

Leverage your passions, talents, and cultural background. Starting from your strengths gives your business authenticity and purpose. For example, I used my love of fashion and culture to build Kaima Designs, and my desire to empower others led me to launch United Colours of Fashion.

2. Validate Your Idea First

Conduct small-scale tests of your product or service (e.g., pop-ups, bazaars, or online). Ask potential customers for feedback. Use surveys, informal interviews, and prototypes to refine your offerings before investing too heavily.

3. Know the Local Landscape

Understand local market demands, customer preferences, and cultural expectations. Research government regulations, tax requirements, and licensing rules for your industry. Tap into local business associations and support networks, such as the Saint John Region Chamber of Commerce, Women in Business New Brunswick, or immigrant business forums.

4. Build a Strong Network

Relationships matter. Connect with mentors, peers, and professionals who understand the local business scene.

Join networking events, incubator programs, or workshops (for example, through ConnexionWorks, the Community Business Development Corporation, or Planet Hatch). Don't be afraid to ask for help. People are often more willing than you think.

5. Understand the Financial Reality

Capital is a major barrier for many immigrant entrepreneurs. Explore microloans and newcomer-focused grants through business development agencies like those mentioned above. Seek not just money, but in-kind support (meaning donations of space, tools, or volunteers) as well. Start lean. Grow gradually to avoid overwhelming financial pressure. Separate personal and business finances early! This is very crucial and will save you money and hours of work during the tax season.

6. Invest in Learning

Attend workshops on business planning, marketing, and accounting. If language is a barrier, seek language support through settlement agencies. Learn about digital tools such as social media, online stores, and payment systems to reach wider audiences.

7. Be Adaptable and Resilient

Rejection and slow starts are normal. Stay flexible and open to adjusting your strategy. Keep learning from feedback, failure, and small wins.

8. Use Your Unique Voice

Your lived experience, culture, and story are your superpowers. Use them in your branding, storytelling, and customer relationships. People connect with authenticity.

9. Maintain a Clear "Why"

Stay grounded in your purpose. Whether it's giving back to your community or creating representation, this will fuel your perseverance.

10. Prioritize Self-Care

Entrepreneurship can be mentally and emotionally demanding. Protect your mental well-being by setting boundaries, celebrating small wins, and seeking support from friends, mentors, and/ or professional counselors.

Kolawole Osundiya (DJ Rossy)
Co-Owner and Director of Events and Marketing,
Crave Merriment, Inc.

I moved to Canada just before the COVID-19 pandemic, having built a solid career in the telecommunications industry in my home country and a side gig in sales consultancy. Becoming an entrepreneur in Canada was not originally part of my plan. It happened out of necessity and a moment of inspiration.

Back then, I enjoyed hosting friends in my house for get-to-gethers filled with music, food, and laughter. When Covid-19 hit and in one of those boring indoor days, I stumbled on a DJ turntable that was for sale online. Music had always been a part of my life. Growing up, my dad had a large collection of different genres. As COVID-19 restrictions became more relaxed, I'd often curate playlists and DJ for my friends using my laptop. So, I bought the turntable and started entertaining myself and friends with it.

Later, I began reaching out to bars, pitching myself not just as a DJ but as someone who could come along with my crowd of supporters. Out of ten venues contacted, only one of them gave me a chance.

After COVID restrictions were lifted, I started hosting monthly Afrobeat events. Interest grew quickly, and within a year, people were requesting weekly events. Seeing a gap in the market for Afrobeat and international music, I teamed up with my business partner, Charles Nwachukwu, and we opened our own space, called Crave Lounge. The launch was successful, but, as with any new venture, we faced many challenges.

Our dream was to create a New York–style lounge, but we ran into regulatory hurdles that limited what we could do. Then came another opportunity: to buy a restaurant. Although it was unfamiliar terrain for us, we decided to take a leap of faith, leaning on our Crave Lounge experience.

Running an existing business came with its own set of complications—from managing staff to addressing cultural issues such as loudness that made some customers uncomfortable.

My Suggestions for You

- **Understand regulations early.** From building permits to fire marshal approvals, not having the proper paperwork can delay your launch or shut you down depending on your kind of business. For example, I couldn't use a regular dishwasher in the lounge due to compliance requirements.

- **Hire right.** It's hard as a newcomer to identify reliable skilled staff. We often hired people we didn't know well, and minor misunderstandings led to resignations, leaving gaps which were difficult to fill quickly because of the limited skill pool.

- **Expect some stereotyping.** It is a rather common misperception that all immigrants are penniless and receive "free money" from the government. This mistaken belief can negatively impact local patronage of immigrant-owned businesses.

- **Get necessary licenses and certifications ahead of time.** For example, we needed the appropriate licenses to sell alcohol, hire bouncers, and manage public gatherings legally.

- **Be disciplined about finances.** Watch your overhead. Go lean at the beginning. We made the mistake of entering partnerships and trying to scale up too early.

- **Research the market.** Saint John is a legacy city with well-established businesses, loyal customers, and economies of scale that newcomers can't compete with easily. Thorough research will help you to navigate this sensitive cultural reality.

- **Focus on your business.** Doing business only when it's convenient won't get you far. Being in business requires total dedication and focus.

- **Prepare for the credit economy.** If you are coming from a cash-based economy, adjusting to Canada's credit-based financial system may be tough. Lenders won't lend to people with no credit history, so we couldn't get a credit card or a business loan and had to rely on personal savings for a time.

- **Networking and Mentorship:** Building a network helped. ConnexionWorks and Uptown Saint John Inc. were invaluable in providing mentorship and helping us navigate the business landscape.

Final Thoughts

Starting a business as a newcomer is hard. Regulations, lack of credit history, and unfamiliar systems make it nearly impossible to dive in immediately. Often, you need to work a traditional job and build financial stability first. That may diminish your energy for entrepreneurship, especially when you are juggling family, jobs, and survival.

There were times we had full bookings but lacked funds for inventory. Other times, cultural mismatches, such as music and unfamiliar jokes, alienated potential customers.

Even the cost of operations is higher for newcomers. Rent for new business is set at a market rate, unlike legacy businesses which enjoy favorable long-tenure leases. And how about wage pressures, low margins, and the temptation to serve only your own community? The chance of burnout is high, but with resilience, success is sure.

Through it all, the lesson is clear: **Don't give up.** Learn, adapt, and build strategically. And most importantly, step out of your cultural bubble. Build a business that resonates beyond your nationality and speaks to the community around you.

Ayo Olaogun
Co-Owner, Nig Partners, Inc. (NPI)

I arrived in Canada with my family in April 2018 after we received our permanent residency. We chose to settle in Saint John, New Brunswick, drawn by its warm and welcoming community. Shortly after our arrival, I enrolled in the MBA program at the University of New Brunswick, Saint John. As I adapted to our new environment, I transitioned to part-time studies to balance work and education.

I joined Greenergy Fuels Canada, initially as an accounts receivable analyst, later advancing to the role of senior finance and credit risk analyst. While I was grateful for the professional growth, I always had a strong desire to build something of my own. At one point, I considered driving for DoorDash in the evenings to earn additional income, but I quickly realized that would be investing time and effort into building someone else's vision. That insight sparked the idea of starting my own delivery business. This led me to purchase a cargo van and begin offering delivery and moving services during evenings and weekends. In 2021, I reconnected with a family friend—Shamsudeen, fondly known as Shams—who was already involved in exporting vehicles to Nigeria. We explored ways to align our interests, and in 2022 we decided to grow an existing venture, Nig Partners Inc., into a broader enterprise. Together, we expanded our offerings to include local deliveries, vehicle shipping, a licensed auto garage, auto sales, U-Haul rentals, and vehicle dismantling.

Our first significant challenge was securing a suitable location zoned for our type of business. Once we found a space, we discovered that to operate as a dealership, we needed to be affiliated with a licensed auto garage. After reaching out to multiple garages without success, we made the bold decision to establish our own licensed facility.

We were advised that setting up an auto garage could take up to one or two years. With determination and diligence, we were able to launch and obtain inspection center licensing within just three months. Yet, the hurdles didn't end there. As newcomers to the industry, we found that gaining the trust of the local community was difficult. Our earliest clients were mostly friends and acquaintances. To pay staff salaries and operational costs, we had to supplement our income by buying, repairing, and reselling vehicles locally. We also faced challenges such as unrealistic pricing expectations from customers, complex regulatory compliance procedures, and the slow process of building credibility in a competitive market. Nonetheless, we remained committed to our vision and kept moving forward.

My Advice to Immigrant Entrepreneurs

1. **Do your research.** Don't assume that what worked in your previous environment will apply here. Understand the new market. Regulations, customer behavior, and business culture may differ. Be curious! Ask questions, read extensively, and seek expert insights.

2. **Find a mentor.** A mentor can offer invaluable guidance. Whether an experienced immigrant or a local entrepreneur, the right mentor can help you navigate industry regulations and avoid costly errors.

3. **Expect setbacks.** You'll likely encounter rejections and bureaucratic delays. Our application for an LMIA to become a designated employer was initially denied. But with persistence and additional documentation, we got our approval within ten weeks. Be resilient.

4. **Understand regulatory demands.** Certain industries are tightly regulated. Take the time to understand the requirements early on. Engage professionals who can help you stay compliant and prepared.

5. **Start with a strong funding plan.** Many financial institutions hesitate to fund new businesses. Be prepared to bootstrap and run lean operations initially. Don't let the lack of funding stall your progress.

6. **Build for the broader market.** Avoid focusing solely on your own ethnic or cultural community. True growth comes from serving a diverse customer base. Today, most of our clients are from Caucasian and Latino communities.

7. **Don't let race define your journey.** Discrimination, where it exists, can be disheartening—but don't allow it to derail your vision. Avoid dwelling on it or using it as an excuse. Let your excellence, consistency, and professionalism speak louder than bias. Trust is earned—and, once earned, it opens doors.

Final Thoughts

Canada is a land of opportunity, but success doesn't come automatically. It takes hard work, resilience, and strategic thinking. If you're an immigrant entrepreneur, don't treat your business as a fallback plan—commit to it wholeheartedly. With the right mindset, mentorship, and integrity, your dream is within reach.

Chisom Ezeh
Founder and CEO, The Publishing Pad, Inc.

On the first day of January 2021, I landed in Canada filled with a mix of excitement and anxiety as I began my MBA program at the University of New Brunswick. More than once, I questioned my decision to leave the familiar for the unfamiliar. But one thing comforted me: the belief that God had gone ahead of me. As a Christian family, we had sought God's guidance and were convinced this was the path He wanted us to take. Still, that didn't make the journey any easier.

At the end of my twelve-month program, like many other immigrants, I joined the Canadian workforce starting from the bottom. Honestly, I was okay with starting over and growing from scratch. But I had a friend who questioned my decision to leave all my years of experience behind. So, alongside my full-time job, I began freelancing as an editor on Upwork.

Landing that first project was tough. Even though my profile said I was based in Canada, many potential clients would first ask where I was originally from. When I mentioned Nigeria, they often didn't return. Many times, I wanted to give up. But I had a strong community that wouldn't let me quit. Eventually, I began to see in myself what they saw in me.

Today, that freelance gig has grown into a full-blown book publishing company that helps coaches, business owners, and other experts package their knowledge, expertise, and legacy into books people actually want to read. In June 2024, I left my full-time job to focus on building The Publishing Pad. From having zero clients to supporting over one hundred clients, publishing more than two hundred books, winning multiple awards, and stepping into rooms I once only dreamed of, I've seen what's possible.

The immigrant's dream is real and attainable. You can build a thriving business and make an impact, wherever you are. The journey may be tough. The beginning may be hard, but hang in there. I can assure you it gets better if you persevere.

I hope my story encourages you to believe that you can be anything you want to be in a new land if you have the right mindset, the right people around you, and a dream bigger than yourself.

A Few Other Tips I'd Love to Share

1. **It's okay to start outside your field** while you find your footing. Just make sure you're working behind the scenes to get to where you need to be. That part-time job is only a stepping stone. Don't become so comfortable that your dream becomes someone else's.

2. **Invest in building quality relationships.** As immigrants, we'll face imposter syndrome and second-guess our decisions many times. In those moments, self-talk alone may not be enough. You need people who will lift you up when you have no strength left.

3. **Be visible.** No matter how good you or your product is, no one will notice if you're not visible. Use social media, attend events, and talk about what you offer. It may take time, but with consistency, the right people will find you.

4. **Don't stop learning.** There's always a better way to do things. Stay teachable. Ask the right questions, seek mentorship, and commit to providing value to your mentor so they'll continue investing in you.

5. **Bet on yourself.** Starting a business in a new country is a big dream, but look around. Other immigrants are thriving. You can, too, but only if you believe you can.

6. **Do things afraid.** Leaving a job I loved to build a business I love wasn't easy. I had doubts, fears, and financial worries. But I knew in my heart it was time, and I stepped out anyway, committing my journey to God. It's turned out to be one of the best decisions of my life. You can do it, too. Just keep moving, even when you're afraid.

I'll leave you with something a baseball coach named Del Howard said a long time ago that still applies today: "If you think you can, you can. If you think you can't, you can't."

See you on the other side of growth and progress.

Agunbiade Seun Richards
Founder, Ministry of Entrepreneurs, and GEN (Global Entrepreneurship Network) Ambassador for Canada

When my family and I arrived in Canada in 2018, I carried with me two suitcases—one filled with winter clothes, the other filled with dreams. I had lived and worked in Dubai, leading teams for multinational IT companies like Acer, Toshiba, Asus, and Kaspersky. I thought I understood business. But nothing quite prepared me for the unique challenges of building a company from scratch as a newcomer in a foreign land.

My first venture in Canada, *Door2Door Pickup Couriers*, started as a university project during my doctoral studies in Entrepreneurship, Innovation, and Sustainability at the University of New Brunswick. The idea was simple: provide a zero-emission delivery service to meet growing e-commerce needs while tackling environmental concerns. But "simple" in theory became "complex" in practice.

The first challenge was **credibility**. As an immigrant, I had no established reputation in the Canadian market. When I approached potential partners and clients, I was often met with polite skepticism: *"We'll think about it."* It wasn't prejudice in the obvious sense—it was the reality that trust is earned over time. My response was to start small, serve exceptionally, and let results speak. One early breakthrough came during the 2020 pandemic when we offered free delivery to international students, immigrant families and immunocompromised residents of Saint John. The glowing feedback from those first clients and the acknowledgement from the Mayor of the City of Saint John became the social proof that opened doors to bigger contracts.

The second obstacle was **navigating the system**—regulations, permits, insurance, taxes, funding applications. Back home, I had instinctively known how to navigate the bureaucracy. Here, every form felt like it was written in a language I didn't speak, and I'm fluent in English! I made it a rule to never leave an information gap unattended. I spent evenings attending free business clinics, connecting with economic development agencies, and calling government helplines until processes became second nature.

Then came **financial constraints**. Traditional funding was almost impossible without a Canadian credit history or collateral. Instead of dwelling on what I didn't have, I leveraged what I did—networks and visibility. I pitched relentlessly at entrepreneurship competitions, often winning seed grants that kept the business alive in the early days. We reinvested profits wisely and embraced a lean, innovative approach.

There were also **cultural adjustments**. In Canada, relationships are often built over time rather than through aggressive business pitches. I learned to slow down, listen more, and adapt my leadership style. Leading diverse teams meant respecting different work cultures, communication patterns, and decision-making styles. That adaptability later became a strength that allowed me to build cohesive, high-performing teams.

Most importantly, I relied on **community**. I co-founded the Black Business Professional Network (BBPN) to create a platform where immigrant entrepreneurs could find mentorship, share resources, and build collaborations. Giving back to others in similar shoes gave me perspective and resilience.

Looking back, my journey can be summarized in three lessons:

1. **Start small, but start now**—credibility grows with consistent, excellent service.

2. **Study the system**—treat learning regulations and local practices as part of your business model.

3. **Build and lean on community**—no one thrives alone.

Door2Door has been recognized for its environmental impact and community contributions. I've won awards, mentored entrepreneurs, and been nominated for national as well as global recognitions. But those achievements are not just mine—they are proof that, with persistence, adaptability, and faith, an immigrant entrepreneur can turn challenges into stepping stones.

The most profound lesson I learned was the power of ecosystems. Success in Canada isn't built in isolation; it thrives in networks. I actively sought out mentorship, attended local entrepreneur meetups, and connected with organizations supporting immigrant entrepreneurs. Those connections not only provided practical guidance but also created opportunities I could never have accessed alone.

Today, looking back, I see that every challenge was a stepping stone. The delays taught me patience. The skepticism sharpened my value proposition. The funding constraints forced creativity. And the cultural learning curve expanded my worldview and business acumen.

My journey didn't stop with Door2Door Pickup Couriers. I have continued to build on these lessons in other roles. I serve as the **GEN (Global Entrepreneurship Network) Ambassa-**

dor for Canada, where I connect and empower entrepreneurs globally. I lecture at universities across Canada, including the University of Victoria, British Columbia, teaching marketing, career preparation, and entrepreneurship, as well as mentoring student entrepreneurs at the University of Calgary, Alberta. Most importantly, I launched the **Ministry of Entrepreneurs**, a non-profit dedicated to educating, coaching, and mentoring under-privileged individuals in Canada—helping them not just dream, but build sustainable futures through enterprise.

If there's one takeaway from my story, it's this: As an immigrant, your uniqueness is not a disadvantage—it's your competitive edge. The very challenges you face can become the raw material for building something extraordinary.

Closing Reflection

Despite the challenges, many immigrants find a way to succeed through resilience, innovation, and adaptability. They bring fresh perspectives, global experience, and a hunger to thrive that fuels their entrepreneurial journey. Understanding the hurdles you face is the first step in overcoming them, and with the right support and strategy, immigrant entrepreneurs can not only succeed in Canada but also enrich its economy and culture in the process.

To every immigrant feeling exhausted from the demands of owning a business, remember you are not alone. With patience, genuine effort, and an open mind, you can thrive in Canada's dynamic business world.

"When you build a business, you're not just creating income. You're creating impact, identity, and independence."
—Daniel Opoku

CHAPTER TEN

Giving Back

*"Pay it forward. A single act of kindness
can create an endless ripple."*
—Anonymous

I find nothing more fulfilling than putting a smile on the face of another
person. I was raised by my parents, extended family, and community with
soul-touching kindness and support. So, it became almost second nature for
me to lend a helping hand wherever I could. Moreover, the Holy Bible teaches
me to love my neighbor as myself (Matthew 22:39).

Volunteering has been one of the most impactful parts of my journey in
Canada. Even when I was new and didn't have local connections, I felt called
to contribute my knowledge and experiences to support various community
programs and activities.

One of my first stops was the Saint John Newcomers Centre. I recalled the
afternoon I walked in as a newcomer seeking guidance, only to soon find
myself volunteering at events and supporting others like me. That experience

was transformative. It taught me that I didn't have to wait to be "settled" before contributing. I could start where I was, with what I had. If you are a newcomer, the same could be true for you. Being settled is relative, and even if it is taking longer than you expected, you can still help somebody else on their journey. Who knows—while supporting others, your own answers may come.

I also got involved at RiverCross Church, where I experienced the kindness of a diverse, and welcoming community. Helping with church activities gave me a sense of purpose and stability, and it reminded me that faith and service often go hand in hand.

At the University of New Brunswick, I joined student-led associations that not only sharpened my leadership skills but also introduced me to peers from all over the world, including members of university management. These connections helped me see Canada not just as a destination, but as a journey shared with others. I later volunteered in the mentorship program.

Joining the Saint John Toastmasters Club was another turning point. I had always known the value of effective communication, but Toastmasters gave me the platform to enhance my confidence, improve my public speaking, and find my voice in a new cultural context. Every speech, every meeting pushed me outside my comfort zone, and that's where real growth happens.

Then there was the Nigerian-Canadian Association of New Brunswick (NCANB). This is a place that feels like home away from home. Volunteering with NCANB helped me stay connected to my roots while contributing to the growth of the Nigerian community in New Brunswick. I saw firsthand how community building and cultural pride can coexist with integration and progress.

Through these opportunities, I gained much more than "Canadian experience." I gained friendships, mentorship, clarity, and a sense of identity in my new country. Volunteering reminded me that even when I was new, unsure, or in transition, I still had value to offer. And giving back, in turn, gave me the confidence to move forward.

If you are a newcomer to Canada, you've likely heard that volunteering is a great way to gain Canadian experience. This is true across many countries. But more than just checking a box, volunteering should be meaningful to your journey.

Volunteering should also be compatible with your well-being. You don't have to say yes to every opportunity that comes your way. In fact, you shouldn't. Focus on programs or organizations that align with your values, interests, and long-term goals. Are you passionate about education, youth development, healthcare, culture, or public speaking? Choose those causes that energize you. When you care about what you're doing, you'll learn faster, build genuine connections, and stay motivated.

It's essential to strike a healthy balance. Many newcomers juggle school, work, family responsibilities, and the emotional demands of settling into a new environment. Volunteering should complement your life, not overwhelm it. Start small, perhaps a few hours a week, and increase your commitment only when it feels manageable.

Think of volunteering as a two-way street. Yes, you are giving your time, but you're also gaining experience, confidence, community, and exposure to the new culture. It's an investment in yourself. Sometimes, the relationships you build through volunteering could lead to jobs, mentorship, or even lifelong friendships. Remember, it's okay to pause or say no sometimes. Your health, stability, and peace of mind come first. The goal is not to be everywhere, but to be present and purposeful where you choose to serve. When volunteering is done with intention, it can open doors, build bridges, and anchor you in your new community.

Key Takeaways

1. You Always Have Something to Offer

You don't need local experience or a perfect résumé to make a difference. Your time, perspective, and willingness to help are enough. We all carry skills and stories that can uplift others. Giving from where you are today creates space for growth, connection, and purpose tomorrow. If you're second-guessing yourself or wondering how you can possibly have anything to offer when you barely know your way around, I understand how that feels, because I was once there. Trust me: what you have is more than enough.

2. Purpose Brings Joy

There's a special kind of fulfillment that comes from giving your time to something bigger than yourself. Volunteering gave me joy, stability, and a sense of belonging that no job or paycheck could provide. It gave my days meaning and turned ordinary moments into impactful memories. When I stopped focusing on what I lacked and started giving what I had, joy followed. Volunteer to do what you love to do, and watch how joyful your life becomes.

3. Relationships Are Sometimes More Valuable than Résumés

Many of my most meaningful Canadian relationships began through volunteering. Volunteering introduced me to people who saw my potential beyond bullet points on a résumé. I met mentors, colleagues, and friends not through job applications, but through shared service. For instance, at Toastmasters club, I met Jim Kokocki, the 2015–2016 Toastmasters International president. Jim Kokocki is a renowned writer, speaker, speech coach and a Distinguished Toastmaster. He would later be an early reader of my manuscript and made meaningful suggestions. Sometimes employers feel more comfortable hiring people they know and trust, or people who have been recommended by someone they know and trust. A good word from the right person can carry more weight than a list of qualifications. That's why building genuine relationships through service, community involvement, or simple human kindness is sometimes the most powerful step you can take toward success in a new country.

4. Leadership Has Many Faces

I learned that leadership doesn't always come with a title. You don't need a formal role to make an impact. You just need to be dependable, courageous, and kind. Leadership is staying after an event to clean up, checking in on someone who's struggling, or bringing ideas forward when no one else does. Volunteering showed me that leaders are those who serve first and inspire by example. Leadership starts when you choose to act instead of standing by. Serving others can help you discover passions and values you didn't know you had. Over time, these small acts will earn respect and open doors you never imagined.

5. Boundaries Are Important

When I first began volunteering, I wanted to help everywhere, so I said yes to many things. But I quickly realized that giving too much of myself without rest leads to burnout. Many newcomers feel the pressure to say yes to every opportunity that comes their way, thinking it will help them settle faster. But volunteering should not be about spreading yourself thin just to be seen. It should be intentional. You don't have to volunteer for everything. You only need to get involved in causes or organizations that align with your values and your passions. I had to learn to set healthy boundaries, not just to protect my time but to honor my other priorities like work, family, and mental health. Saying "no" doesn't mean you're not committed; it means you're making your contribution sustainable. You serve best when you are rested, focused, and intentional. Boundaries aren't selfish. They're necessary for long-term impact and personal growth. Balance matters!

Closing Reflection

To anyone starting out, don't wait until you feel ready to volunteer. Serve where you are. Say yes to the right causes, then show up. You could offer your time, your voice, your presence, your smile or even your shoulder for someone else to lean on. The relationships you build, the skills you sharpen, and the character you develop will be worth far more than you can imagine. If you have received kindness and support in your lifetime, paying it forward is probably the greatest way to appreciate such kindness.

"The best way to find yourself is to lose yourself in the service of others."
—Mahatma Gandhi

Your Journey, Your Legacy

Stepping into a new land, whether in business, academics, career, family, or any other new endeavor, is more than a physical relocation. It is a journey of the soul, the mind, and the spirit. As you've seen throughout this book, being an immigrant or newcomer is not a setback and should never be viewed as such. It is a strategic decision rooted in courage, sacrifice, and a vision for a better future.

Yes, there are challenges. The unfamiliarity, the culture shock, the uncertainties, and the occasional feelings of isolation can be overwhelming. However, within every obstacle lies an opportunity to grow, learn, and thrive. Cast your vision by painting the picture of your ideal life. Learn effective time management, and cultivate resilience. These are not just motivational slogans; they are your tools. Your blueprint. Your daily compass.

Resilience is not just for the strongest among us. Asking questions when you discover that you don't know something is a form of resilience. Believing you can overcome challenges—that, too, is resilience. After a challenging moment or even a failure, find out what you didn't know, then try again. Your resilience is your superpower. Every challenge you face is shared in some ways by millions of others walking a similar path. Every victory you achieve becomes part of a greater story: a story of courage, contribution, and transformation.

Your family, your children, and your cultural heritage are not burdens. They are your grounding force. They are the bridges between who you were, who you are, and who you are becoming. Hold onto them as you

navigate and integrate. Let your values enrich your new environment even as you adapt to its rhythms.

Networking and deliberate integration will open doors, many of which you didn't even know existed. The relationships you build now can become life-lines, mentors, business partners, or simply friends who make the journey lighter. In the workplace, remember that you bring value. Learn the unspoken rules, be confident, and adapt, but always believe in your worth.

Finally, never forget to give back once you are in a place to do so. When you rise, lift others. Your story can be someone else's inspiration. Your journey, with all its trials and triumphs, becomes part of a collective legacy that shapes the newcomer narrative for future generations.

It is your journey. Own it, shape it, and never forget that you have the power to turn your experience into a lasting legacy. Your experiences are valid. Your struggles are real, but so are your potential and your triumphs.

This is not the end of your story. It is just the beginning. Continue to dream boldly, act intentionally, and live purposefully. You are a strategic immigrant, and your best is yet to come.

About the Author

From wiring electrical systems to rewiring mindsets, **Isaac O. Ebhohimhen** is a dynamic leader who blends technical expertise with a deep passion for personal growth and transformation. With degrees in electrical and electronics engineering, operations and production management, university teaching, and an international MBA from Canada, Isaac's journey from Lagos, Nigeria, to North America is a testament to grit, grace, and growth.

Isaac has over a decade of international experience in project and operations management across industries including energy, IT, supply chain, and facilities management. He has led and supported projects in Africa, the United States, Dubai, the United Kingdom, and now Canada, where he currently works as a project manager.

Beyond the boardroom, Isaac is a passionate motivational speaker, career coach, and mentor to immigrants and newcomers. He is deeply committed to helping others navigate change with clarity, strategy, and faith. His work is guided by Christian values, cultural intelligence, and a belief that no journey is wasted when lived with purpose.

Whether he's managing complex projects, mentoring future leaders, or spending quality time with his family, Isaac leads with intention and heart. This book is his heartfelt contribution to fellow newcomers and immigrants, lighting the path with practical wisdom and lived experience so others can thrive in unfamiliar places without stumbling in the dark.

To connect with Isaac O. Ebhohimhen,

Email: isaacebhohimhen@gmail.com
Facebook: isaac.ebhohimhen
Instagram: @yenrovwo

Reviews

"The Strategic Newcomer is more than a guide; it's a heartfelt, courageous, and genuine resource for anyone navigating any new beginning. Through raw story-telling, actionable strategies, and wisdom, Isaac captures the emotional complexity of the immigrant journey with grace and authenticity. His humility, clarity, and inclusion of diverse voices make this standout work. This book is a powerful companion for thriving, belonging, and becoming. Isaac is a wonderful, thoughtful, intentional, and driven human, with an inspiring attitude and approach to life and service to others. He is a tremendous force for impact, and anyone who knows him is better for it."

—Glen Fillmore

Vice President, Strategic Growth and Transformation, Saint John Energy.

"A perfect blend of heartfelt narrative and practical strategy, The Strategic Newcomer is the essential guide for any professional starting a new chapter. Isaac's empathetic and motivational voice provides clear, step-by-step advice on networking and integration that feels both personal and authoritative. This book doesn't just help you land; it ensures you thrive. It's the perfect carry-on for a successful journey, making sure you don't just arrive, but truly take off in your career."

—Chris Weir

Sales and Business Development Professional | MBA Sales Instructor | Axis Co-founder and Sales Coach in Residence

"Isaac O. Ebhohimhen has written an important book that would serve newcomers as a survival guide. Isaac shares personal stories, both his and other newcomers', offering valuable insights and reflections. This book is moving, as the author writes with empathy and deep understanding drawn from his and other newcomers' experiences. It will also be useful to cultural humility coaches as a reference material, providing perspective on the significant sacrifices newcomers make to successfully integrate in new countries and offering options for bridging the gap."
—**Sochi Azuh**
Podcaster & Communication Specialist | Saint John Newcomers Centre

"The Strategic Newcomer is a practical and inspiring guide for newcomers to Canada, offering thoughtful insights into thriving beyond the immigration process. With honesty and wisdom, the author addresses the emotional, spiritual, and professional adjustments that come after landing. Grounded in faith and personal experience, the book equips readers to navigate identity, purpose, and integration with intentionality. It moves beyond survival, encouraging immigrants to embrace growth, community impact, and long-term fulfillment. With no doubt, The Strategic Newcomer is an excellent resource for individuals and families seeking to not only settle but flourish in their new environment."
—**Pastor William Folarin Onososen**
Senior Pastor, Redeemed Christian Church of God, Saint John

"The Strategic Newcomer is the personal story of the immigration experience, with a clear passion to help others facing a similar adventure. The book captures the many obstacles all individuals and families must accept when adapting to a new culture while also being honest about the less obvious inner work—the mental and emotional adjustments that is required. What I loved most about this book is the genuine desire to support others through the actionable advice on nearly every page. This should be a mandatory reading for anyone immigrating. It's the mentor every newcomer deserves."
—**Rev. Rob Nylen**
Senior Pastor, RiverCross Church

"In The Strategic Newcomer, Isaac O. Ebhohimhen delivers more than a guide. He offers a lifeline to all immigrants. He invites you to see yourself not as a displaced person, but as divinely strategically positioned. This book is a practical and heartfelt blueprint for navigating life after relocation. Each page provides you with tools for thriving, truths for healing, and reminds you that the immigrant journey is not just about survival but about becoming. Isaac's The Strategic Newcomer is a much-needed voice in a world that often overlooks the quiet strength of those starting over. This is a gift many immigrants didn't know they needed but will be so glad they found."

—Sophia Etuhube

Award-winning Journalist | Coach | Mentor

"This is a tremendous resource for employers, community leaders, newcomers, and anyone interested in assisting newcomers acclimatize to a new environment, especially in a smaller town or city."

—Jim Kokocki

2015-2016 International President, Toastmasters International

"I was delighted when Isaac asked me to review his manuscript. As a newcomer, I could immediately relate to his story—the confusions and struggles of walking into a world of uncertainty when you have pretty much lived a settled life in a country you have known forever. The most captivating part of the book was Isaac's inclusion of other newcomer experiences along with his own, which gives many perspectives. I am sure each reader will be able to find their own story in it. "The key takeaways and strategies he used to overcome his struggles are an important part of the book. It made me recall all the steps I took when I was looking for a house, a part-time job, volunteering opportunities, which was a concept so new to me, and even creating my own new social circle. We have all sailed the same ship as we weave our own unique experience.

"Another part of the book that stood out for me was an entire chapter dedicated to creating a solid foundation for the family to navigate the challenges of a new country. I loved Isaac's strategic approach to helping his children adapt and settle in a new social and educational environment. Many parents struggle with it, trying to balance work alongside their own emotional battles with the aim of providing their families the abundant life they uprooted them for.

"Overall, it was a nostalgic read for me and I am sure it will be for many of the readers. Thank you, Isaac, for writing this book. It will be an invaluable source of inspiration for many of us who are here and the many who will come after us."
—Celeste Dean

www.ingramcontent.com/pod-product-compliance
Lightning Source LLC
Chambersburg PA
CBHW071406120626
46546CB00002B/831